THE BUST OF SHAKESPEARE AT STRATFORD-ON-AVON
See page 32

SHAKESPEARE

The Man and his Stage

AMS PRESS
NEW YORK

SHAKESPEARE
The Man and his Stage

By

E. A. G. LAMBORN

and

G. B. HARRISON

LONDON
OXFORD UNIVERSITY PRESS
HUMPHREY MILFORD
1923

Library of Congress Cataloging in Publication Data

Lamborn, Edmund Arnold Greening, 1877-
    Shakespeare, the man and his stage.

    Original ed. issued in series: The World's manuals.
    1.   Shakespeare, William, 1564-1616--Biography.
2.   Shakespeare, William, 1564-1616--Stage history--
To 1625. I. Harrison, George Bagshawe, 1894-
joint author. II. Title. III. Series: The World's
manuals.
PR2894.L3   1973   822.3'3   73-153336
ISBN 0-404-03805-0

This reprint has been authorized by the Clarendon Press,
Oxford, England

Reprinted from the edition of 1923, Oxford
First AMS edition published in 1973
Manufactured in the United States of America

AMS PRESS INC.
NEW YORK, N. Y.   10003

The Life

In the Register of Baptisms at Holy Trinity Church, Stratford, may be read the transcript made in 1600 of the original record which has now vanished,

'1564, April 26 Gulielmus filius Johannes Shakspere.'

There is no record of Shakespeare's birth, but as the practice was to baptize the child within a few days the common belief that the birthday was 23rd April may be correct. Neither is it known certainly in what house he was born; but on 29th April 1552, as the town records tell, John Shakespeare was fined 12*d*. for making a 'sterquinarium' or heap of refuse before the door of his house in 'Hendley Strete'; and in 1575 he bought for £40 from Edmund Hall the house in that street now called the Birthplace, which may therefore have been the place where his children were born.

Their names, as entered in the Stratford register, are a long list, in which William comes third:

Joan, baptized 15th September 1558.
Margaret, baptized 2nd December 1562.
William.
Gilbert, baptized 13th October 1566.
Joan, baptized 15th April 1569, the elder Joan being dead.
Anne, baptized 28th September 1571.
Richard, baptized 11th March 1574.
Edmund, baptized 3rd May 1580.

Their father is called a glover in the town records of a suit brought against him by Thomas Siche in 1556 for a debt of £8; but he also dealt in corn, for in the same year he sued Henry

Fyld to recover 18 quarters of barley or its price. In extracts presently to be quoted he is called a butcher and a dealer in wool. As a farmer he would engage in all those trades ; but he seems to have had too many irons in the fire, for in the end he lost his money and fell into debt.

However, at the time of William's birth he was a rising tradesman. He had married, probably in 1557, Mary the youngest

STRATFORD.　The house in which Shakespeare was born.　From Malone's
Supplement to Shakespeare's Plays, 1780

daughter of Robert Arden, whose will, dated November 1556, is preserved in the Registry Court at Worcester. It shows that he was a small landowner of Wilmcote in the parish of Aston Cantlow, and it gives his land there, called Asbies, to his daughter Mary. Now though Mary probably could not write, for when she mortgaged Asbies in 1579 she put her mark to the deed instead of signing her name, it is believed that she had been brought up in gentle society and that Shakespeare's gentility owed much to her. ' For gentle blood doth gentle manners breed.'

He went, we are told, to the free school of his native town, which any Stratford boy who had learned to read might attend. What he would learn there would be to converse in Latin, to decline his noun and his verb from Lilly's Latin Grammar, and to read extracts from Ovid and a few other Latin writers. One of the most popular (among schoolmasters) was Baptista Spagnolo of Mantua (1448–1516), whose Eclogues, written in imitation of

STRATFORD. The Grammar School

Virgil, are quoted by Holofernes in *Love's Labour's Lost*— when Shakespeare's memories of him were still fresh. But the comment 'Good old Mantuan!' expresses the pedagogue's sentiments rather than the poet's.

In the eight years during which he might have attended it, Stratford School had no less than five head masters. Little is known of any of them ; the very name of the one who stayed longest has been forgotten, though it is recorded that he came from Warwick Grammar School, which was then one of the best in England. Shakespeare evidently felt that he owed no gratitude to any of them, for he never mentions a schoolmaster except to make fun of him, which suggests that he did not remain long enough at school to realize that even a schoolmaster has blood in his veins ' and will bleed if you prick him '.

When he entered the school, probably at the age of seven in 1571, his father was at the height of his prosperity. Entries in the Record Books of the Town Council show that John Shakespeare was for several years one of the most active and influential members of that body; after holding various other important offices he became high bailiff or mayor in 1568, and now in 1571 he was elected chief alderman and so, incidentally, by the custom of the time, became entitled to the dignity of a grant of arms, which he afterwards claimed. But about the time when his son most needed schooling, at the age of fourteen or so, the Stratford records tell a different story, and suggest that William Shakespeare was taken away from school because his father could not afford to keep him there any longer.

They show that John Shakespeare was no longer a regular attendant at the Council meetings; that in 1578 he was able to pay only half his alderman's tax towards the maintenance of the Queen's army, and in 1579 nothing; that he could not pay his ' poor rate ', being evidently so poor himself that the council agreed he should ' not be taxed to paye anythynge '. The will of Roger Sadler, a Stratford baker, dated November 1578 mentions a debt of £5 due from ' Mr. John Shaksper', which suggests that he could not even pay for his children's bread. He had sold his wife's property at Snitterfield and mortgaged her land of Asbies; and now, like Dickens's father in aftertime, he may have taken his son from school to make him work for the younger children.

At this point the Shakespeare family fall under a cloud in more than one sense; the records fail us for several years and we have to depend upon stories and traditions collected after Shakespeare's death by the admirers of his works. Of these the most industrious was Nicholas Rowe, who in 1709 published an edition of *The Works* and prefixed to it 'Some Account of the Life, &c., of Mr. William Shakespear', much of which was told him by Betterton, the actor, who had spent some time in Stratford collecting the local traditions of the poet, and had talked of him with Sir William Davenant, Shakespeare's godson. This account states that

'He was the son of Mr. *John Shakespear*, and was born at *Stratford* upon *Avon*, in *Warwickshire*, in *April* 1564. His family, as appears by the Register and other publick Writings relating to that Town, were of good figure and fashion there, and are mention'd as gentlemen. His father, who was a considerable dealer in wool, had so large a family, ten children in all, that, tho' he was his eldest son, he could give him no better education than his own employment. He had bred him, 'tis true, for some time at a Free-school, where 'tis probable he acquir'd that little *Latin* he was master of : But the narrowness of his circumstances, and the want of his assistance at home, forc'd his father to withdraw him from thence, and unhappily prevented his further proficiency in that language.'

Another account of these obscure years is given in some earlier notes for a 'Life' written in the reign of Charles II by John Aubrey, a gentleman of a family now represented by Sir Lancelot Aubrey Fletcher of Boarstall, who loved to collect gossip and scandal, and wrote 'Brief Lives' of many famous people. He was, as his friend Anthony Wood remarked, 'magotieheaded and exceedingly credulous', and many of his stories are apocryphal, but what he says of Shakespeare may be true. Among Wood's papers in the Bodleian Library is a letter from Aubrey written when he was collecting information about Shakespeare : 'Did I tell you that I have met with old Mr. Beeston who knew all the old English poets, whose lives I am taking from him : his father was master of the . . . playhouse.' In his life of Beeston, Aubrey adds that the old man had gained his knowledge of Shakespeare from an actor named Lacy, who had known him.

' His father was a butcher,[1] and I have been told heretofore by some of the neighbours, that when he was a boy he exercised his father's trade, but when he kill'd a calfe, he would doe it in a high style, and make a speech. There was at the time another butcher's son in this towne, that was held not at all inferior to him for a naturall witt, his acquaintance and coetanean, but dyed young.'

At the end of 1582, when Shakespeare was 18, the cloud lifts for a moment and gives us a glimpse of him. In the registry office of the bishop of the diocese there was discovered in 1836 a bond dated 28th November 1582, signed by two Stratford farmers, declaring ' that William Shagspere one thone partie, and Anne Hathwey of Stratford, in the dioces of Worcester, maiden, may lawfully solemnize marriage together '. Such a document would enable them to obtain a licence to be married without waiting for the usual calling of the banns, and in Advent, when marriage in ordinary circumstances was forbidden. Where and when the marriage took place is not known, but the Stratford register of baptisms records ' 1583, May 26th, Susannah, daughter to William Shakspere '. The inscription on Anne's tombstone tells us that she died in August 1623, aged 67 ; at the date of the marriage therefore she was 26.

In February 1585, according to the Stratford register, ' Hamnet and Judith, sonne and daughter to William Shakespere ', were baptized, which suggests that Shakespeare and his wife were still living at Stratford. An entry in the records of the Town Council shows that his father's affairs had gone from bad to worse : he is deprived of his aldermanship because ' he doth not come to the halles nor hath he of long time '. Then the cloud falls again darker and more impenetrable than ever, and except for traditional stories we learn no more of Shakespeare until 1592.[2]

[1] It was not uncommon at this time for a tradesman to combine several interests.

[2] Except that in 1589 he was joined with his parents in a lawsuit tried in the Court of Queen's Bench. His father's numerous lawsuits help to explain the legal knowledge shown in many of the plays.

These stories, however, agree with what we should expect to hear of a young man like Shakespeare in such circumstances as those in which we have just left him.

' Upon his leaving school, he seems to have given intirely into that way of living which his father propos'd to him ; and, in order to settle in the world after a family manner, he thought fit to marry while he was yet very young. His wife was the daughter

CHARLECOTE GATE HOUSE

of one *Hathaway*, said to have been a substantial yeoman in the neighbourhood of *Stratford*. In this kind of settlement he continu'd for some time, 'till an extravagance that he was guilty of forc'd him both out of his country, and that way of living which he had taken up ; and tho' it seemed at first to be a blemish upon his good manners, and a misfortune to him, yet it afterwards prov'd the occasion of exerting one of the greatest *Genius's* that ever was known in dramatick Poetry. He had, by a misfortune common enough to young fellows, fallen into ill company ; and amongst them, some that made a frequent practice of Deer-stealing, engag'd him more than once in the robbing a park that belong'd to Sir *Thomas Lucy*, of *Cherlecot*, near *Stratford*. For this he was prosecuted by that gentleman,

as he thought, somewhat too severely; and in order to revenge
that ill usage, he made a ballad upon him. And tho' this,
probably the first essay of his Poetry, be lost, yet it is said to have
been so very bitter that it redoubled the prosecution against him
to that degree, that he was oblig'd to leave his business and
family in *Warwickshire*, for some time, and shelter himself in
London.

' It is at this time, and upon this accident, that he is said to
have made his first acquaintance in the Play-house. He was
receiv'd into the Company then in being, at first in a very mean
rank; but his admirable wit, and the natural turn of it to the
stage, soon distinguish'd him, if not as an extraordinary actor,
yet as an excellent writer. His name is printed, as the custom
was in those times, amongst those of the other Players, before
some old Plays, but without any particular account of what sort
of parts he us'd to play; and tho' I have inquir'd, I could never
meet with any further account of him this way, than that the top
of his performance was the ghost in his own *Hamlet.*' Thus Rowe.

Aubrey's account is:

' This William being inclined naturally to poetry and acting,
came to London, I guesse, about 18; and was an actor at one of
the playhouses, and did act exceedingly well (now B. Johnson
was never a good actor but an excellent instructor).

' He began early to make essayes at dramatique poetry, which
at that time was very lowe; and his playes tooke well.

' He was a handsome, well shap't man: very good company,
and of a very readie and pleasant smooth witt. . . .

' Though, as Ben: Johnson sayes of him, that he had but little
Latine and lesse Greek, he understood Latine pretty well, for
he had been in his younger yeares a Schoolmaster in the countrey
—from Mr. Beeston.'

Dr. Johnson records a story which Sir William Davenant had
told Betterton, who had passed it on to Rowe and Rowe to Pope:

' In the time of Elizabeth, coaches being yet uncommon, and
hired coaches not at all in use, those who were too proud, too
tender, or too idle to walk, went on horseback to any distant
business or diversion. Many came on horseback to the play,
and when Shakespere fled to London from the terror of a

criminal prosecution, his first expedient was to wait at the door of the playhouse and hold the horses of those that had no servants, that they might be ready again after the performance. In this office he became so conspicuous for his care and readiness, that in a short time every man, as he alighted, called for Will. Shakespere, and scarcely any other waiter was trusted with a horse, while Will. Shakespere could be had. This was the first dawn of better fortune. Shakespere finding more horses put into his hand than he could hold, hired boys to wait under his inspection, who, when Will. Shakespere was summoned, were immediately to present themselves, *"I am Shakespere's boy, sir!"* In time Shakespere found higher employment; but as long as the practise of riding to the playhouse continued, the waiters that held the horses retained the application of *Shakespere's boys.'*

According to Malone, who wrote in 1780,

' There is a stage tradition, that his first office in the theatre was that of prompter's attendant; whose employment it is to give the performers notice to be ready to enter as often as the business of the play requires their appearance on the stage.'

William Oldys (1696–1761) records a tradition that

' One of Shakespere's younger brothers, who lived to a good old age, even some years, as I compute, after the restoration of *King Charles II*, would, in his younger days, come to London, to visit his brother *Will*, as he called him and be a spectator of him as an actor in some of his own plays. This custom, as his brother's fame enlarged, and his dramatick entertainments grew the greatest support of our principal, if not of all our theatres, he continued it seems so long after his brother's death, as even to the latter end of his own life. The curiosity at this time of the most noted actors to learn something from him of his brother, &c., they justly held him in the highest veneration. And it may be well believed, as there was besides a kinsman and descendant of the family, who was then a celebrated actor. This opportunity made them greedily inquisitive into every little circumstance, more especially in his dramatick character, which his brother could relate of him. But he, it seems, was so stricken in years and, possibly, his memory so weakened with infirmities (which might make him the easier pass for a man of weak intellects) that he could give them but little light into their inquiries; and all that could be recollected from him of his brother *Will* in that station, was the faint, general, and almost lost ideas he had of having once seen him act a part in one of his own comedies, wherein being to personate a decrepid old man, he wore a long beard and appeared so weak and drooping, and unable to walk, that he was forced to be supported and carried by another person to a table, at which he was seated among some company who were eating, and one of them sung a song.' (Presumably the character of Adam, in *As You Like It*, II. vii.)

This account of Shakespeare's fortune-finding in London is curiously like the story of another Stratford youth who was his contemporary, one John Sadler, ' who join'd himself to a carrier, and came to London where he had never been before, and sold his horse in Smithfield, and having no acquaintance in London to recommend him or assist him went from street to street and house to house asking if they wanted an apprentice. . . .' At last he persuaded a grocer named Brokebank to take him as apprentice and became eventually a successful tradesman.

Another ' acquaintance and coetanean ' of Shakespeare who came from Stratford to make his fortune in London was Richard Field, son of a Stratford tanner, who printed Shakespeare's first published work, and afterwards became Master of the Stationers' Company.

Shakespeare no doubt was naturally attracted to the London stage and he may even have known some persons connected with it, for the Stratford Corporation accounts show that his father in the days of his prosperity had used his official position to encourage players to give performances in the town. Indeed it has been suggested that Shakespeare seized the opportunity offered by a visit of the Earl of Leicester's company to Stratford in 1587 to attach himself to them and to get himself taken up to London on their return.

In 1592 the cloud lifts again, and we see enough to confirm the truth of much in these stories; Shakespeare is a prosperous actor and a popular playwright. The proof of his prosperity is that he has made friends and enemies ; two of them in that year speak as follows—the enemy first.

He is Robert Greene, a Cambridge scholar. On his death-bed, worn out prematurely by evil living, he writes a warning to his playwriting friends and calls it *A Groatsworth of Wit bought with a Million of Repentance.*

' Base minded men al three of you, if by my miserie ye be not warned : for unto none of you (like me) sought those burres to cleave ; those Puppits (I meane) that speake from our mouths, those Anticks garnisht in our colours. . . . . Yes, trust them not : for there is an upstart Crow, beautified with our feathers, that with his *Tygers heart wrapt in a Players hide,* supposes he is as well able to bumbast out a blanke verse as the best of you ; and being an absolute *Iohannes fac totum,* is in his owne conceit the onely Shake-scene in a countrie. O that I might intreate your rare wits to be imployed in more profitable courses : & let those Apes imitate your past excellence, and never more acquaint them with your admired inventions. I know the best husband of you all will never prove an Usurer, and the kindest of them all will neuer proove a kinde nurse ; yet whilst you may, seeke you better Maisters ; for it is pittie men of such rare wits, should be subject to the pleasures of such rude groomes.'

The italicized remark ' Tygers heart wrapt in a Players hide ' is a reference to *3 Henry VI*, i. v. 137, and, coupled with the name ' Shake-scene ' leaves little doubt as to who was meant.

This effusion of envy was published after Greene's death by Henry Chettle, a printer and author who was a friend of the dead man. But Shakespeare's friends must have protested against the injustice done to him ; for in publishing his *Kind Hart's Dreame* shortly afterwards Chettle took the opportunity in the Preface to apologize, admitting that what he had himself seen of Shakespeare as well as common report of him proved Greene's charges to be slanderous.

' About three moneths since died M. Robert Greene, leaving many papers in sundry Booke sellers hands, among other his Groatsworth of wit, in which, a letter written to divers play-

makers, is offensively by one or two of them taken, and because
on the dead they cannot be avenged, they wilfully forge in their
conceites a living author : and after tossing it to and fro, no
remedy, but it must light on me. How I have, all the time of
my conversing in printing, hindred the bitter inveying against
schollers, it hath been very well knowne ; and how in that I dealt
I can sufficiently proove. With neither of them that take offence
was I acquainted, and with one of them I care not if I never be :
the other, whome at that time I did not so much spare, as since
I wish I had, for that as I have moderated the heate of liuing
writers, and might have usde my owne discretion (especially in
such a case) the author beeing dead, that I did not, I am as sory,
as if the originall fault had beene my fault, because myselfe have
seene his demeanor no lesse civill, than he exelent in the qualitie
he professes : besides, divers of worship have reported his
uprightness of dealing, which argues his honesty, and his facetious
grace in writting, that aprooves his art.'

What Shakespeare had written ' that approved his art ' by
1592 is uncertain ; the play containing the line parodied by
Greene was not then published in print, and is now believed to
be only in part Shakespeare's. But in the next year begins a
series of records that make us henceforth independent of
traditions for our knowledge of his work and its rewards. The
registers preserved by the Stationers' Company record the issue
of the licence for the printing of *Venus and Adonis* in 1593 and
of *Lucrece* in 1594. And the Dedications prefixed to those poems,
the second particularly, prove that Shakespeare had won for
himself the esteem of one of the greatest lords in the kingdom,
Henry Wriothesley, Earl of Southampton. He speaks so warmly
of his patron that we are inclined to believe the following story
told by Rowe—though the sum mentioned must be exaggerated :

' He had the honour to meet with many great and uncommon
marks of favour and friendship from the earl of *Southampton*,
famous in the histories of that time for his friendship to the
unfortunate earl of *Essex*. It was to that noble Lord that he
dedicated his Poem of *Venus and Adonis*. There is one instance
so singular in the magnificence of this Patron of Shakespear's,

that if I had not been assur'd that the story was handed down by Sir *William D'Avenant*, who was probably very well acquainted with his affairs, I should not have ventur'd to have inserted, that my lord *Southampton* at one time gave him a thousand pounds,

to enable him to go through with a purchase which he heard he had a mind to. A bounty very great, and very rare at any time, and almost equal to that profuse generosity the present age hath shewn to *French* Dancers and *Italian* Singers.'

At any rate by 1596 he had money to spare to fee the Heralds for assigning a coat of arms to his father. The draft of the grant at the Heralds' College is dated Oct. 20th, 1596. Just at that time his only son Hamnet died and was buried, as the burial register shows, at Stratford.

' 1596, August 11th, Hamnet, filius William Shakespere.'

Perhaps for this reason that he had now no son to inherit them, he did not then trouble further

HENRY WRIOTHESLEY
third Earl of Southampton

about the arms, which were not formally granted until 1599. But early in the following year he bought for £60 the largest house in his native town, New Place, built by that Sir Hugh Clopton who had been Lord Mayor of London and the restorer of Stratford bridge, as his arms, with those of London, remaining upon it testify.

Further evidence of his growing wealth is found in letters that have come down to us written by Stratford people who wished

FACSIMILE OF THE LETTER FROM RICHARD QUYNEY TO SHAKESPEARE

to borrow money from him—a proof of prosperity almost as convincing as the offer to lend.   One of them, found by Malone in 1793 among the Corporation Records and now in the Stratford Museum, is from Richard Quyney, a vintner, whose son afterwards married his daughter Judith.

' Loveinge Contreyman, I am bolde of yow as of a Frende, craveinge yowr helpe with xxxll, uppon Mr. Bushells and my securytee, or Mr. Myttons with me.   Mr. Rosswell is nott come to London as yeate, and I have especiall cawse.   Yow shall Frende me muche in helpeing me out of all the debettes I owe in London, I thanck God, and muche quiet my mynde, which wolde nott be indebeted.   I am nowe towardes the Cowrte, in hope of answer for the dispatche of my Buysenes.   Yow shall nether loase creddytt nor monney by me, the Lorde wyllinge ; and nowe butt perswade yowr selfe soe as I hope, and yow shall nott need to feare, butt, with all hartie thanckefullnes, I wyll holde my tyme and content yowr Frende, and yf we Bargaine farther yow shalbe the paiemaster yowr selfe.   My tyme biddes me hasten to an ende, and soe I committ thys [to] yowr care and hope of yowr helpe.   I feare I shall nott be backe thys night From the Cowrte.   Haste.   The Lorde be with yow and with us all, amen.   From the Bell in Carter Lane, the 25 octobr 1596.

Yowrs in all kyndenes,
Ryc. Quyney.

' To my Loveinge good Frend
     and contreyman Mr. Wm.
     Shackespere deliver thees.'

But since a man is known by the company he keeps it is important to note that Shakespeare's friends included not only earls on the one hand and country tradesmen on the other, but also the greatest writers of his time.   The most famous was Ben Jonson, of whose first acquaintance with him the following story is told by Rowe :

' His acquaintance with *Ben Johnson* began with a remarkable piece of humanity and good nature; Mr *Johnson*, who was at that time altogether unknown to the world, had offer'd one of his Plays to the Players in order to have it acted; and the persons into whose hands it was put, after having turn'd it carelesly and superciliously over, were just upon returning it to him with an ill-natur'd answer, that it would be of no service to their Company; when *Shakespear* luckily cast his eye upon it, and found something so well in it as to engage him first to read it through, and afterwards to recommend Mr *Johnson* and his writings to the publick.'

Shakespeare's association with Jonson afterwards became very close; in 1598 he acted in his friend's comedy *Every Man in his Humour*, and there are many traditions of their private friendship, a picturesque account of which is given by Fuller in *The Worthies of England*, 1662.

Jonson regarded himself as the first playwriter of the age, but a passage in a contemporary play called *The Return from Parnassus* (1600) shows that Shakespeare, even before his greatest plays were written, was looked upon as his superior in genius if not in learning. One actor, Kemp, is made to say to another:

' Few of the university pen plaies well, they smell too much of that writer *Ovid*, and that writer *Metamorphosis*, and talke too much of *Proserpina* and *Juppiter*. Why here's our fellow *Shakespeare* puts them all downe, I and *Ben Jonson* too. O that *Ben Jonson* is a pestilent fellow, he brought up *Horace* giving the Poets a pill, but our fellow *Shakespeare* hath given him a purge that made him beray his credit.' ' Its a shrewd fellow indeed,' answers Burbage.

Leonard Digges,[1] too, in some verses prefixed to an edition of the *Poems* brought out in 1640, drew a similar comparison between the plays of the two poets:

So have I seen, when *Caesar* would appeare,
And on the stage at halfe-sword parley were

[1] See also p. 40.

Brutus and *Cassius* : oh how the Audience
Were ravish'd, with what new wonder they went thence,
When some new day they would not brooke a line
Of tedious (though well laboured) *Catiline* ;
Sejanus too was irkesome, they priz'de more
Honest *Iago*, or the jealous Moore . . .

Another admirer was Francis Meres, who in his *Palladis Tamia,
Wits Treasury*, published in 1598, wrote :

' As the Greeke tongue is made famous and eloquent by *Homer,
Hesiod, Euripides, Aeschylus, Sophocles, Pindarus, Phocylides,*
and *Aristophanes* ; and the Latine tongue by *Virgill, Ovid,
Horace, Silius Italicus, Lucanus, Lucretius, Ausonius,* and *Clau-
dianus* ; so the English tongue is mightily enriched and gorgeously
invested in rare ornaments and resplendent abiliments by
*Sir Philip Sidney, Spenser, Daniel, Drayton, Warner, Shakespeare,
Marlowe* and *Chapman.*—As the soule of *Euphorbus* was thought
to live in *Pythagoras* : so the sweete wittie soule of *Ovid* lives
in mellifluous and hony-tongued *Shakespeare,* witnes his *Venus
and Adonis,* his *Lucrece,* his sugred Sonnets among his private
friends, &c,—As *Plautus* and *Seneca* are accounted the best
for Comedy and Tragedy among the Latins : so *Shakespeare*
among yᵉ English is the most excellent in both kinds for the
stage ; for Comedy, witnes his *Gentlemen of Verona,* his *Errors,*
his *Love Labors Lost,* his *Love Labours Wonne,* his *Midsummers
night dreame,* and his *Merchant of Venice* : for Tragedy his
Richard the 2, *Richard the* 3, *Henry the* 4, *King John, Titus
Andronicus,* and his *Romeo and Juliet.* As Epius Stolo said that
the Muses would speake with Plautus tongue if they would speak
Latin : so I say that the Muses would speak with Shakespeare's
fine filed phrase if they would speak English. . . .'

But more flattering still is the evidence that Shakespeare's
work had won for him the admiration of the great Queen herself.
In the accounts kept by the Treasurer of the Chamber there is
a record of the payment ' to William Kempe, William Shakespeare
and Richarde Burbage servauntes to the Lord Chamberleyne,
upon the Councelles warrant dated at Whitehall xvᵗᵒ Marcij,
1594, for twoe severall Comedies or Enterludes shewed by them

before her majestie in Christmas tyme laste paste, viz, upon St. Stephens daye and Innocentes daye xiij^{ll} vj^{s} viij^{d} and by waye of her majesties Rewarde vj^{li} xiiij^{s} iij^{d}, in all xx^{li}.' There are several similar records in succeeding years, and tradition has always held that she was so taken by Falstaff in the play of *Henry IV* that she asked his creator to write another play showing him in love. In Rowe's account of the story (it came through Dryden from Davenant) :

‘ Queen *Elizabeth* had several of his Plays acted before her, and without doubt gave him many gracious marks of her favour. It is that maiden princess plainly, whom he intends by a—*A fair vestal, throned by the west* [*Midsummer Night's Dream*]. And that whole passage is a compliment very properly brought in, and very handsomly apply'd to her. She was so well pleas'd with that admirable character of *Falstaff*, in the two parts of *Henry the fourth*, that she commanded him to continue it for one Play more, and to show him in love. This is said to be the occasion of his writing *The Merry Wives of* Windsor. How well she was obey'd, the play itself is an admirable proof. Upon this occasion it may not be improper to observe, that this part of Falstaff is said to have been written originally under the name of *Oldcastle* [see the Epilogue to *2 Henry IV*]. Some of that family being then remaining, the Queen was pleas'd to command him to alter it ; upon which he made use of *Falstaff*. The present offence was indeed avoided ; but I don't know whether the Author may not have been somewhat to blame in his second choice, since it is certain that Sir *John Falstaff* [Fastolfe], who was a Knight of the garter, and a Lieutenant-general, was a name of distinguish'd merit in the wars in *France* in *Henry* the fifth's and Henry the sixth's times. What grace soever the Queen conferr'd upon him, it was not to her only he ow'd the fortune which the reputation of his wit made.'

When James I succeeded to the throne one of his first acts upon arriving in his new capital was to issue 17th May 1603, a licence

‘ to these our servants Laurence Fletcher, William Shakespeare, Richard Burbage, Augustine Phillippes, John Hemmings,

Henrie Condell, William Sly, Robert Armyn, Richard Cowlye
and the rest of their associats, freely to use and exercise the
Arte and facultie of playing Comedies, Tragedies, Histories,
Enterludes, Moralls, Pastorals, Stage-plaies and such other like . . .
as well for the recreation of our loving subjects as for our solace
and pleasure, when we shall thinke good to see them. . . .   To
show and exercise publiquely to their best Commoditie . . . as well
within theire now usuall howse called the Globe . . . as also within
anie towne halls, or Mout halls, or other convenient places within
the liberties and freedome of any other Cittie, Universitie,
Towne or Borough whatsoever within our said Realmes and
dominions.'

When the king entered London in state the next year Shakespeare was one of those in attendance, if not in his train, and
'The Accompte of Sir George Howne, Knight, Master of the
Greate Warederobe' shows that he received 4½ yards of 'skarlet
red cloth' for a dress upon that occasion. It is interesting to
observe that his monument at Stratford shows him in a doublet
of scarlet cloth.

A bundle of documents discovered in the Record Office a few
years ago by Professor C. W. Wallace gives us a glimpse of Shakespeare at this time living in his London lodgings as a friend of
the family with whom he boarded. The papers are the record
of a lawsuit brought by a theatrical costume-maker named
Stephen Bellott against his father-in-law Christopher Mountjoy,
a wigmaker of Silver Street. Bellott had been apprentice to
Mountjoy, and had married his daughter Mary about 1605. In
1612 he quarrelled with his father-in-law, declaring that a dowry
of £50 had been promised and not paid, and bringing an action
to recover it, 7th May 1612. Many witnesses gave evidence,
which was duly written down by the clerks of the court; and
among these writings the deposition of

'Wm. Shakespeare of Stratford upon Aven in the Countye of
Warwicke gentleman of the age of XLVIII yeres or thereaboutes
sworne and examined the day and yere abovesaid (11th May

1612) deposethe and sayethe . . . he Knowethe the partyes
plaintiff and deffendant and hathe knowne them bothe as he
nowe remembrethe for the space of tenne yeares or thereaboutes. . . .' (He goes on to prove that Bellott had been an
industrious and valuable apprentice and that he had often heard
the question of his marriage discussed in the family.) 'And
further this deponent sayethe that the said deffendantes wyeffe
did sollicitt and entreat this deponent to move and perswade the
said complainant to effect the said marriadge and accordingly this
deponent did move and persuade the Complainant thereunto.'

And so he signs the deposition with the first of his six signatures
that remain for us.

His evidence was corroborated by the deposition of one Daniel
Nicholas.

'This deponnent sayth he herd one Wm. Shakespeare saye that
the defendant did beare A good oppinion of the plaintiff and
affected him well when he served him. And did move the
plaintiff by him the said Shakespeare to have a marriadge betweene
his daughter Marye Mountioie and the plaintiff. And for that
purpose sent him the said Shakespeare to the plaintiff to perswade the plaintiff to the same as Shakespere told him this
deponnent which was effected and solempnized uppon promise of
a porcion with her. . . . The deponnent sayth that the plaintiff
did requeste him this deponnent to goe with his wyffe to Shakespeare to understande the truthe how muche and what the
defendant did promise to bestowe on his daughter in marriadge
with him the plaintiff. And askinge Shakespeare therof he
Answered that he promised if the plaintiff would marrye with
Marye his the defendantes onlye daughter he the defendant
would by his promise as he Remembered geve the plaintiff with
her in marriadge about the some of ffyftye pounds in money and
Certayne Houshould stuffe.'

Other witnesses also refer to Shakespeare's part in the business and to their conversations with him ; and his connexion with the parties is explained by a reference in the deposition of Joan Johnson, a servant of Mountjoy's, to ' one Mr. Shakespeare that lay [i. e. lodged] in the house' at the time when the marriage was arranged.

The case was not settled by the Court but was referred to the heads of the French Protestant Church in London. From this, and from other evidence, e. g. the copy of his naturalization certificate 27th May 1607, we learn that Mountjoy was a Huguenot who had taken refuge in London and set up in business like many of his countrymen. If Shakespeare was lodging with him when he wrote *Henry V* he would have learned, perhaps from Mary Mountjoy, how to make a French girl like Catherine talk to her lover.

' Silver Street ', wrote Stow about this time, ' is, I think, of Silver smiths dwelling there, in which be divers fair houses. And on the north side thereof is Monkswell Street.' And on the corner, where now is a tavern, stood the Mountjoy's house, a ' fair ' one no doubt, for the wigmaker was clearly well to do. And here Shakespeare once lodged.

The rest of his story, so far as it can be read in the records, is one of continued good fortune. In the worldly sense, at least, Shakespeare had become, and remained till his death, a prosperous and wealthy man. The numerous documentary references to him that have come down to us are mainly concerned with property he bought, money he sued for in the courts, or plays of his which were acted or published. All tell the same tale of his growing wealth and reputation. From documents preserved in the Stratford Museum we learn that on May-day 1602 he bought for £320 from William and John Combe 107 acres of arable land in Old Stratford ; and later in the same year a house near New Place of one Walter Gatley and another of Hercules Underhill of Stratford. In 1604 he paid £440 for a 32 years' lease of half the Stratford tithes, which brought in at least £60 a year and moreover gave him the right of burial in the chancel of his church. Other documents record his purchase of a house in Blackfriars, London, in March 1613, and of more property at Stratford. These possessions made Shakespeare one of the most important men in his native town, as is proved by letters written by the town clerk in 1614, when there was a proposal to enclose some of the common lands of Stratford. They show that he was consulted at every step, and received ' the coppyes of all our acts and also a not [note] of the inconvenyences wold happen by the inclosure '. He told the town clerk ' that he was not able to beare the enclosing of Welcombe ', and he seems to have succeeded in preventing it.

Besides all this property he owned a large share in the theatre in which his plays were acted, as we learn from a Petition in the Record Office, dated 1635, addressed to ' the Rt. Hon. Philip Earle of Pembroke and Montgomery Lord Chamberlain of his Majesties household ' by

' Cutbert Burbage and Winifred his brother's wife and William his sonne . . . humbly shewing . . . how the father of us Cutbert and Richard Burbage was the first builder of playhowses . . . and built this house [The Theatre] upon leased ground by which meanes the landlord and hee had a great suite in law, and, by his death the like troubles fell on us his sonnes : we then bethought us of altering from thence, and at like expence built the Globe . . . and to ourselves wee joyned those deserveing men Shakspere, Hemings, Condall, Phillips, and others, partners in the profittes of that they call the House.'

The dates of the plays and some contemporary references to them will be discussed in another chapter. Here something must be said upon the question whether they themselves do not tell a story of Shakespeare's spiritual life very different from that of the material prosperity told in the documentary records.

No one can read them without observing that those known to be earliest are full of light-hearted fun and high spirits ; that in the latest, though the rollicking laughter is silent, there is ever present a kindly smile and a gentle heart ; but that the plays of the middle period are instinct with bitterness and scorn, as if they had been written by one whose heart had been outraged and his faith in human goodness shaken by treachery and wrong.

In reading *Romeo and Juliet*, for example, we may weep over the woes of the hapless lovers, yet we leave the play with no sense of the littleness of human life but rather with the feeling that so to love and die together is to triumph over death and fate ; since in the end all must die we no more regret Romeo and Juliet than we sorrow for Wolfe dead in the moment of victory. So, in spite of all the suffering of Hermione and the roguery of Autolycus, we leave the *Winter's Tale* with our hearts braced by the assurance that all man's inhumanity to man does but reveal man's unconquerable mind, that not even the worst of men is irretrievably wicked, and that in Shakespeare's own incomparable words, ' there is some soul of goodness in things evil '. But in such a play as *Troilus*, as in Mr. Hardy's *Jude*, we are made to doubt humanity itself, to conclude

> That hope is all a lie,
> And faith a form of bigotry,
> And love a snare.

Even in the awful tragedy of *Lear* death comes like night and sleep to knit up the ravelled sleeve of care and bring to tortured hearts peace at the last ; but in these middle-period plays Shakespeare, like his own Barnardine, mocks at death itself as a petty thing,—a terror to fools and cowards indeed, but as hopeless and futile as life, and no solution of life's problems.

It seems impossible not to believe that when these plays were being written Shakespeare had passed through some experience which had changed for the time his outlook on life. There is nothing at all in any record of his time to suggest what that experience may have been. But the mother of bitterness is disappointment ; and since the records all go to prove that Shakespeare must have realized a great part of his worldly

ambitions his sufferings may well have been from the keener if
briefer pangs of despised love—' the travails and torments of
love forlorne or ill bestowed, either by disgrace, deniall, delay,
and twenty other wayes, that well experienced lovers could
recite ', as his contemporary Puttenham wrote. Some think that
they have found the clue in the *Sonnets*. These were published
without Shakespeare's leave or knowledge, probably by some one
who had stolen copies of them, in 1609 ; but some, at least, had
been written before 1598, when Meres referred to ' his sugred
sonnets among his private friends.'. How and where the thief
got hold of them is as much a mystery as why they were written
and to whom.

They speak of passionate love, of jealousy, remorse, and self-
contempt, of weariness and discontent with life. They have
been supposed by some to show that Shakespeare was once
ensnared by some evil but brilliant and fascinating woman like
his own Cleopatra. This is not the only story that has been read
into them. Some believe that the sonnets, like the plays, do not
tell Shakespeare's own story, but only his experience of human
life,—that they are imaginative creations, and no more the actual
records of Shakespeare's guilty love than Macbeth is of his
criminal ambition, or Timon of his treatment by the world.

The question, like all questions worth asking, can never be
definitely answered in this world. And that is its fascination.

One thing is fairly certain, that Shakespeare in his later years
enjoyed all that makes life happy, ' as honour, love, obedience,
troops of friends '. As the stories now to be quoted show, he
retired to his pleasant house at Stratford as a man of fortune and
lived there with his wife and daughter, saw his children's children,
and kept the friends of his own youth.

The varied record of his father's chequered life had ended in
1601 with the simple entry in the Stratford burial register :

' Sept. 8   Mr. Johanes Shakspeare '.

His mother ' Mayry Shaxpere, Wydowe ' lived until September

1608. His elder daughter, Susanna, had married in 1607 Dr. John Hall, a famous physician; she lived at Stratford, and her daughter Elizabeth, Shakespeare's only grandchild, was born there and baptized in the parish church on the 21st February in the next year. His younger daughter Judith no doubt lived with her mother at New Place.

'The latter part of his life was spent, as all men of good sense will wish theirs may be, in ease, retirement, and the conversation of his friends. He had the good fortune to gather an estate equal to his occasion, and, in that, to his wish; and is said to have spent some years before his death at his native Stratford. His pleasureable wit and good nature engag'd him in the acquaintance and entitled him to the friendship of the gentlemen of the neighbourhood.' (Rowe.)

Early in 1616 Judith Shakespeare was married to Thomas Quiney, the Stratford wine-merchant's son, and about the same time her father made his will, now preserved at Somerset House. It fills three sheets of paper, and is too long to quote. By it he left almost all his property to his eldest daughter for her life, afterwards for her son if she should have one, and, if not, to Judith's son. Eventually, in default of male heirs, it passed to Susanna's daughter Elizabeth, at whose death in 1670 Shakespeare's line ended and his property was scattered among various legatees. The mystery of the will is the omission of any reference to his wife, except in a single sentence interpolated as an afterthought by which he leaves her his second-best bed. The law would give her a certain income for life out of her husband's property, but he gave her nothing beyond this, not even the use in her widowhood of the house of which she had been mistress as his wife. Many explanations have been suggested, but all are guesses.

A brief account of these last days is given us in a memorandum made by the Rev. John Ward when he became Vicar of Stratford in 1662:

'Shakespear had but two daughters, one whereof Mr. Hall,

the physitian, married, and by her had one daughter, to wit, the Lady Bernard of Abbingdon. I have heard that Mr. Shakespeare was a natural wit, without any art at all; hee frequented the plays all his younger time, but in his elder days lived at Stratford, and supplied the stage with two plays every year, and for that had an allowance so large that hee spent att the rate of a thousand a yeer, as I have heard.—Shakespear, Drayton and Ben Jhonson, had a merry meeting, and, itt seems, drank too hard, for Shakespear died of a feavour there contracted.[1]—Remember to peruse Shakespears plays and bee versed in them, that I may not bee ignorant in that matter.'

Other evidence at once of Shakespeare's hospitality and of the variety in his acquaintanceship is given in a record in the Corporation Accounts at Stratford under the date 1614 : 'Item : for one quart of sack and one quart of clarett wine, geven to a preacher at the Newe Place, xx^d '—the usual present from the Corporation to a visiting minister who had preached before them on the previous Sunday.

On the 25th April 1616 Ward's predecessor, Richard Watts, buried Shakespeare in the chancel of his parish church, and entered his burial in the register :

'1616, Aprill 25. Wtt Shakspeare gent.'

It is said that the grave was dug seventeen feet deep.

No name was inscribed upon the ledger stone that covered it—only the lines traditionally said to have been prepared by him before his death in order that his bones might not be dug up, according to the custom of the time, and removed to the charnel-house to make room for new burials :

GOOD FREND FOR IESUS SAKE FORBEARE,
TO DIGG THE DUST ENCLOASED HEARE :
BLESTE BE $\overset{E}{Y}$ MAN $\overset{T}{Y}$ SPARES THES STONES,
AND CURST BE HE $\overset{T}{Y}$ MOVES MY BONES.

The original stone having become crumbled and worn was

---

[1] A note made by another local clergyman, Archdeacon Davies (d. 1708), on a MS. now at Corpus Christi College, Oxford, says that 'he dyed a papist'.

THE CHANCEL, STRATFORD-ON-AVON CHURCH

replaced in 1830 by the present one, upon which the inscription was copied.

Before 1623, when Ben Jonson mentions it, a monument was set up on the north wall of the chancel above the grave. Sculptors who have examined the bust are agreed that the head was modelled from a mask of the face taken for the purpose in wax or plaster after death. Sir William Dugdale, a Warwickshire man, noted in his diary, 1653, that 'Shakespeares and John Combes monum^{ts}, at Stratford sup' Avon [were] made by one Gerard Johnson'. But Shakespeare's has several times been repaired and repainted—once in 1748 by John Hall, a 'limmer' of Stratford, and after it had been whitewashed by Malone in 1793 it was repainted in its present colours by Collins of London in 1851. The epitaph (see frontispiece) was probably written by Dr. Hall, who was a capable scholar.

Dr. Hall was not, however, so accomplished as a herald, for the shield above the bust shows only the arms that John Shakespeare had obtained in 1599, not quartered, as they should have been, with Mary Arden's coat; and on his own tombstone, also, the arms are wrongly arranged, and do not agree with the inscription that ' he married Susanna ye daughter *and co-heire* of Will. Shakespeare, Gent.', for the Shakespeare coat is impaled, not quartered. His own son-in-law, Thomas Nashe, however, knew better and, as may be seen on his gravestone, quartered Shakespeare's arms with his own, as he was entitled to do through his marriage with the poet's only grandchild.

In 1693 a person named Dowdall visited Stratford, and in a letter to his friend, Mr. Edward Southwell, wrote an account of his conversation with the parish clerk :

' The clarke that shew'd me this church is above 80 years old ; he says that this Shakespear was formerly in this towne bound apprentice to a butcher, but that he run from his master to London, and there was received into the playhouse as a serviture, and by this meanes had an oportunity to be what he afterwards prov'd. He was the best of his family, but the male line is extinguish'd. Not one for feare of the curse abovesaid [i. e. on the tombstone] dare touch his gravestone, tho his wife and daughters did earnestly desire to be layd in the same grave with him.'

The Vestry-book at Stratford shows that the clerk and sexton in 1693 was one William Castle; he could not, however, have been as old as Dowdall supposed, for his baptism is entered in the parish register under the date 1628.

Shakespeare's writings are so wonderful that it is something of a shock to pass from a study of the plays to the almost prosaic facts that form our only record of his life. The contrast has been made still more startling by the tendency of modern worshippers to represent the plays as even more marvellous than they really are, and some people have been so staggered by it that, taken off their balance, they have even doubted whether the man whose life appears so ordinary could be the writer of such extraordinary works.

It is, therefore, important to remember that though the men of Shakespeare's own day admired his works, they admired even more the man who wrote them. As all the accounts of him agree in declaring, he was so pleasant spoken, witty, good humoured, and sweet tempered that the large-hearted sympathy with all sorts and conditions of men which amazes us in the plays then surprised nobody : it was what all who knew him expected of him. Even the people who praised his work used epithets that often leave us wondering whether they are meant to apply to the man or his poetry : ' sweet Shakespeare ', says the anonymous author of *Polymanteia* in 1595, agreeing with a character in *The Returne from Parnassus,* who swears ' I'le worshipp sweet Mr. Shakespeare '; ' friendly Shakespeare ' he is called in the preface to Scoloker's *Daiphantus* (1604) ; Webster, in the dedication of his *White Divel* (1612), expresses admiration for his ' right happy and copious industry '. And so when he was dead the first tributes to his memory were inspired no less by love for the man than by admiration of the works he had left behind him.

Thus, when in 1623 his plays were first collected and published in the famous ' first folio ', by Heminge and Condell, his
fellow actors of the Globe, the dedication and the preface written
by these friends voice as eloquently their affection for him as
their commendation of his book.

The dedication, ' To the most noble and incomparable paire
of brethren, William, Earle of Pembroke, and Philip Earle of
Montgomery ', contains the following passages :

' But since your Lordships have beene pleas'd to thinke these
trifles some-thing, heeretofore ; and have prosequuted both them,
and their Authour living, with so much favour : we hope, that
(they out-living him, and he not having the fate, common with
some, to be exequutor to his owne writings) you will use the like
indulgence toward them, you have done unto their parent.
There is a great difference, whether any Booke choose his Patrones,
or finde them : This hath done both. For, so much were your
Lordships likings of the severall parts, when they were acted, as
before they were published, the Volume ask'd to be yours. We
have but collected them, and done an office to the dead, to procure
his Orphanes, Guardians ; without ambition either of selfe-profit,
or fame : onely to keepe the memory of so worthy a Friend, &
Fellow alive, as was our Shakespeare, by humble offer of his
playes, to your most noble patronage. . . . We most humbly
consecrate to your Honours these remaines of your servant
Shakespeare; that what delight is in them, may be ever your
Lordships, the reputation his, & the faults ours, if any be committed, by a payre so carefull to shew their gratitude both to the
living, and the dead, as is

Your Lordshippes most bounden,
John Heminge.
Henry Condell.'

Then follows the remarkable address :

' *To the great Variety of Readers.*

' From the most able, to him that can but spell : There you
are number'd. We had rather you were weighd. Especially,
when the fate of all Bookes depends upon your capacities : and

not of your heads alone, but of your purses. Well! It is now publique, & you will stand for your priviledges wee know : to read, and censure. Do so, but buy it first. That doth best commend a Booke, the Stationer saies. Then, how odde soever your braines be, or your wisedomes, make your licence the same, and spare not. Judge your sixe-pen'orth, your shillings worth, your five shillings worth at a time, or higher, so you rise to the just rates, and welcome. But, what ever you do, Buy. Censure will not drive a Trade, or make the Jacke go. And though you be a Magistrate of wit, and sit on the Stage at *Black-Friers* or the *Cock-pit* to arraigne Playes dailie, know, these Playes have had their triall alreadie, and stood out all Appeales ; and do now come forth quitted rather by a Decree of Court, then any purchas'd Letters of commendation.

' It had bene a thing, we confesse, worthie to have bene wished, that the Author himselfe had liv'd to have set forth and overseen his owne writings ; But since it hath bin ordain'd otherwise, and he by death departed from that right, we pray you do not envie his Friends, the office of their care, and paine, to have collected & publish'd them ; and so to have publish'd them, as where (before) you were abus'd with diverse stolne and surreptitious copies, maimed, and deformed by the frauds and stealthes of injurious impostors, that expos'd them : even those, are now offer'd to your view cur'd, and perfect of their limbes ; and all the rest, absolute in their numbers, as he conceived them. Who, as he was a happie imitator of Nature, was a most gentle expresser of it. His mind and hand went together : And what he thought, he uttered with that easinesse, that wee have scarce received from him a blot in his papers. But it is not our province, who onely gather his works, and give them you, to praise him. It is yours that reade him. And there we hope, to your divers capacities, you will finde enough, both to draw, and hold you : for his wit can no more lie hid, then it could be lost. Reade him, therefore ; and againe, and againe : And if then you doe not like him, surely you are in some manifest danger, not to understand him. And so we leave you to other of his Friends, whom if you need, can bee your guides : if you neede them not, you can leade your selves, and others. And such Readers we wish him.

John Heminge.
Henrie Condell.'

The editors invited Ben Jonson, as Shakespeare's friend and colleague and his acknowledged successor at the head of his profession, to write some commendatory verses to be prefixed to their book. These, as befits their purpose, praise Shakespeare first as a poet, though even in them Jonson slips once or twice into the expression of personal feeling as when he speaks of ' my gentle Shakespeare ' and ' my beloved the author '.

To the memory of my beloved,
The AUTHOR
Mr. William Shakespeare :
And
what he hath left us.

To draw no envy (*Shakespeare*) on thy name,
   Am I thus ample to thy Booke, and Fame :
While I confesse thy writings to be such,
   As neither *Man*, nor *Muse*, can praise too much.
'Tis true, and all mens suffrage. . . .
I, therefore will begin. Soule of the Age !
   The applause ! delight ! the wonder of our Stage !
My *Shakespeare*, rise ; I will not lodge thee by
   Chaucer, or *Spenser*, or bid *Beaumont* lye
A little further, to make thee a roome :
   Thou art a Moniment, without a tombe,
And art alive still, while thy Booke doth live,
   And we have wits to read, and praise to give.
That I not mixe thee so, my braine excuses ;
   I meane with great, but disproportion'd *Muses* :
For, if I thought my judgement were of yeeres,
   I should commit thee surely with thy peeres,
And tell, how farre thou didst our *Lily* out-shine,
   Or sporting *Kid*, or *Marlowes* mighty line.
And though thou hadst small *Latine*, and lesse *Greeke*,
   From thence to honour thee, I would not seeke
For names ; but call forth thund'ring *Æschilus*,
   Euripides, and *Sophocles*, to us,
Paccuvius, *Accius*, him of *Cordova* dead,
   To life againe, to heare thy Buskin tread,

And shake a Stage : Or, when thy Sockes were on,
  Leave thee alone, for the comparison
Of all, that insolent *Greece*, or haughtie *Rome*
  Sent forth, or since did from their ashes come.
Triumph, my *Britaine*, thou hast one to showe,
  To whom all Scenes of *Europe* homage owe.
He was not of an age, but for all time !
  And all the *Muses* still were in their prime,
When like *Apollo* he came forth to warme
  Our eares, or like a *Mercury* to charme !
Nature her selfe was proud of his designes,
  And joy'd to weare the dressing of his lines !
Which were so richly spun, and woven so fit,
  As, since, she will vouchsafe no other Wit.
The merry *Greeke*, tart *Aristophanes*,
  Neat *Terence*, witty *Plautus*, now not please ;
But antiquated, and deserted lye
  As they were not of Natures family.
Yet must I not give Nature all : Thy Art,
  My gentle *Shakespeare*, must enjoy a part.
For though the *Poets* matter, Nature be,
  His Art doth give the fashion. And, that he,
Who casts to write a living line, must sweat,
  (Such as thine are) and strike the second heat
Upon the *Muses* anvile : turne the same,
  (And himselfe with it) that he thinkes to frame ;
Or for the lawrell, he may gaine a scorne,
  For a good *Poet's* made, as well as borne.
And such wert thou. Looke how the fathers face
  Lives in his issue, even so, the race
Of *Shakespeares* minde, and manners brightly shines
  In his well torned, and true-filed lines :
In each of which, he seems to shake a Lance,
  As brandish't at the eyes of Ignorance.
Sweet Swan of *Avon* ! What a sight it were
  To see thee in our waters yet appeare,
And make those flights upon the bankes of *Thames*,
  That so did take *Eliza*, and our *James !*
But stay, I see thee in the *Hemisphere*
  Advanced, and make a Constellation there !

Shine forth, thou Starre of *Poets*, and with rage,
  Or influence, chide, or cheere the drooping Stage;
Which, since thy flight frō hence, hath mourn'd like night.
  And despaires day, but for thy Volumes light.

BEN: IONSON.

But writing afterwards in his *Discoveries* Jonson shows that he

MARTIN DROESHOUT'S ENGRAVING
from the First Folio, 1623

considered his dead friend as even more remarkable for his lovable
nature than for his art:

'*I remember*, the Players have often mentioned it as an honour
to *Shakespeare*, that in his writing, (whatsoever he penn'd) hee
never blotted out a line. My answer hath beene, would he had
blotted a thousand. Which they thought a malevolent speech.
I had not told posterity this, but for their ignorance, who choose
that circumstance to commend their friend by, wherein he
most faulted. And to justifie mine owne candor, (for I lov'd the
man, and doe honour his memory (on this side Idolatry) as much

as any.) Hee was (indeed) honest, and of an open and free nature : had an excellent *Phantsie* ; brave notions, and gentle expressions : wherein hee flow'd with that facility, that sometime it was necessary he should be stop'd : *Sufflaminandus erat ;* as *Augustus* said of *Haterius*. His wit was in his owne power ; would the rule of it had beene so too. Many times hee fell into those things, could not escape laughter : As when hee said in the person of

THE 'DROESHOUT' PAINTING
believed to be the original of Droeshout's engraving

Caesar, one speaking to him ; *Caesar thou dost me wrong*. Hee replyed : *Caesar did never wrong, but with just cause* : and such like ; which were ridiculous. But hee redeemed his vices, with his vertues. There was ever more in him to be praysed, then to be pardoned.'

Again in the lines written by Ben Jonson opposite Shakespeare's portrait on the frontispiece of the Folio it is the personal

qualities of which he thinks first, the gentle manners and the
ready wit :

> This Figure, that thou here seest put,
>   It was for gentle Shakespeare cut ;
> Wherein the Graver had a strife
>   With Nature, to out doo the life :
> O, could he but have drawne his wit
>   As well in brasse, as he hath hit
> His face ; the Print would then surpasse
>   All, that was ever writ in brasse,
> But, since he cannot, Reader, looke,
>   Not on his Picture, but his Booke.

(The picture was drawn by Martin Droeshout, a Dutch engraver,
who, as he was only fifteen at the date of Shakespeare's death,
must have copied another picture; a painting[1] now at Stratford
is believed to be the original of his engraving.)

Jonson, Heminge, and Condell were Shakespeare's ' fellows '
and may be suspected of a natural partiality towards their com-
rade. But there are not wanting tributes to the dead man from
persons in other ranks of life ; one of them was Leonard Digges,
a member of University College, Oxford, son of a baronet and
nephew of a judge. He celebrated at once the publication of
the Folio and the setting up of Shakespeare's monument at
Stratford in the following verses :

> *Shake-speare*, at length thy pious fellowes give
> The world thy Workes : thy Workes, by which, out-live
> Thy Tombe, thy name must : when that stone is rent,
> And Time dissolves thy *Stratford* Moniment,
> Here we alive shall view thee still. This Booke,
> When Brasse and Marble fade, shall make thee looke
> Fresh to all Ages . . . .
> Be sure, our *Shake-speare*, thou canst never dye,
> But crown'd with Lawrell, live eternally.

[1] Reproduced on p. 39, by permission, from the painting in the Memorial
Picture Gallery.

2

Shakespeare's Age

' It was the best of times, it was the worst of times, it was the age of wisdom, it was the age of foolishness, it was the epoch of belief, it was the epoch of unbelief, it was the season of Light, it was the season of Darkness, it was the spring of hope, it was the winter of despair . . .'—at least all these opinions are to be found expressed in its literature. And this diversity of opinion is perhaps the most significant characteristic of the age : in religion, in philosophy, in science, in literature, history, and politics, new ideas were springing into life and struggling with the old. Behind them all, animating and invigorating all, was ' the searching and unsatisfied spirit of the English ', an ardent curiosity, an eager interest in all the possibilities of human experience which led the Elizabethans as it led the Greeks to be ever seeking some new thing.

Men were tempted once more to believe that by eating the fruit of the tree of knowledge they would become as gods. ' The end of our foundation ', said the Father of Salomon's House,[1] ' is the knowledge of causes, and secret motions of things ; and the enlarging of the bounds of human empire, to the effecting of all things possible.'

The spirit of the age is reflected in Shakespeare's rhapsody on the godlike reach of man in *Hamlet* :

' What a piece of work is man ! How noble in reason ! how infinite in faculties, in form and moving ! how express and admirable in action ! how like an angel in apprehension, how like a god ! the beauty of the world ! the paragon of animals ! '

But not even Shakespeare felt this truth more poignantly or

[1] In Bacon's *New Atlantis*.

was moved more eloquently by it than Marlowe. His two greatest
characters, Tamburlaine and Faustus, are inspired by it to grasp
at superhuman powers. Faustus, like Prospero, would wrest
from Nature secrets that should make him her master :

> O what a world of profit and delight,
> Of power, of honour, of omnipotence
> Is promised to the studious artizan !
> All things that move between the quiet poles
> Shall be at my command : Emperors and Kings
> Are but obeyed in their several provinces,
> Nor can they raise the wind, or rend the clouds ;
> But his dominion that exceeds in this,
> Stretcheth as far as doth the mind of man.

So Tamburlaine declares that

> Nature, that fram'd us of four elements
> Warring within our breasts for regiment,
> Doth teach us all to have aspiring minds :
> Our souls, whose faculties can comprehend
> The wondrous architecture of the world,
> And measure every wandering planet's course,
> Still climbing after knowledge infinite,
> And always moving as the restless spheres
> Will us to wear ourselves and never rest.

Chapman, too, in a passage that Shakespeare might have envied,
shows in a picture the adventurous soul of the English renais-
sance :

> Give me a spirit that on this life's rough sea
> Loves t' have his sail filled with a lusty wind
> Even till his sail-yards tremble, his masts crack,
> And his rapt ship runs on her side so low
> That she drinks water, and her keel plows air ;
> There is no danger to the man that knows
> What life and death is : there's not any law
> Exceeds his knowledge ; neither is it lawful
> That he should stoop to any other law.
>   (*Byron's Conspiracy*, Act III.)

But it was not the poets only who held that

> He who made us with such large discourse,
> Looking before and after, gave us not
> That capability and god-like reason
> To fust in us unused ;

the coldly intellectual Bacon, in the first book of his *Advancement of Learning*, wrote what might be a gloss on Marlowe's lines, declaring ' that God hath framed the mind of man as a mirror or glass, capable of the image of the universal world, and joyful to receive the impression thereof, as the eye joyeth to receive light ; and not only delighted in beholding the variety of things and vicissitudes of times, but raised also to find out and discern the ordinances and decrees, which throughout all these changes are infallibly observed . . . for nothing parcel of the world is denied to man's inquiry and invention '.

> Search where thou wilt, and let thy reason go
> To ransom Truth, even to th' Abyss below ;
> Rally the scattered causes, and that line,
> Which Nature twists, be able to untwine.
> It is thy Maker's will, for unto none
> But unto Reason can He e'er be known.

No Elizabethan would have seen anything extravagant in Bacon's great boast, ' I have taken all knowledge to be my province ' : it expressed the ideal of the age. Men ' looked before ', into the future, and saw imaginary commonwealths like Utopia and Atlantis ; they ' looked after ', into the past of the world, and, especially, like Stow and Camden, into the history of their own island ; they looked afar in space as in time, and discovered a new world beyond the horizon ; they looked above, and discovered the rolling of the planets and the insignificance of the earth in comparison with the grasp of their own minds ; they looked, with Shakespeare's help, into those minds themselves, and devised systems of education by which human powers could be developed and increased ; they looked into their own bodies, and discovered the circulation of their blood and the mysteries of their physical origin.

They lit a fire that burns still, more clearly, if less fiercely; for we also consider these things. But they realized as we do not that knowledge is barren until it is rooted in the emotions : all a man's knowledge of a thing is sterile unless it leads him to love the thing of which he learns ; and, unlike ourselves, ' they never forgot that they were animals. They never let any one else forget that they were divine '. To be a good animal yet never to make a beast of yourself was a part of life's philosophy which the Elizabethans, like the Greeks, had learned. ' Learning is but an adjunct of ourself ' : they knew that a man may be as much warped by book-learning alone as by ignorance ; and Shakespeare's obvious admiration for such men as Henry V, which may puzzle the modern student, would have been to them perfectly natural. He knew that learning purchased at the expense of living was a bargain that only a pedant would prize : he valued it only as it made life more interesting.

As one of the characters said in *The Return from Parnassus*, ' A meere scholler is a creature that can strike fire in the morning at his Tinder box, put on a pair of lined slippers, sit rewming till dinner and then go to his meate when the Bell rings, one that hath a peculiar gift in a cough, and a license to spit : or if you will have him defined by negatives, He is one that cannot make a good legge, one that cannot eat a messe of broth cleanly, one that cannot ride a horse without spur galling, one that cannot salute a woman and looke on her directly . . .'

So to the Elizabethans physical education was no less important than intellectual exercise ; and the object of both was increased range and power of enjoyment and self-expression, the pleasures of the cultivated senses no less than of the cultivated mind. This explains the enthusiastic love for music which characterizes the age and which is so conspicuous in Shakespeare : our too bookish education has made us forget that Elizabethan music was as remarkable, and in its own day as famous, as Elizabethan literature. To be able to join in part-singing was an accomplishment expected of every gentleman. One of the numerous writers on music, Thomas Morley, in his *Introduction to Practicall Musicke* (1597), makes a scholar describe how he was asked to join in a song, and ' refusing and pretending ignorance, the whole companie condemned mee of discurtesie. . . . But supper being ended, and Musicke books, according to the custome, being brought to the table, the mistresse of the house presented mee with a part, earnestly requesting mee to sing. But when, after manie excuses, I protested unfainedly that I could not, everieone began to wonder. Yea, some whispered to others demanding how I was brought up.' It is interesting to remember that the musical instruments played by order of Nebuchadnezzar are all given English names in the Authorized Version of the Bible, and represent an orchestra of Shakespeare's day.

The love of gardens and the love of field-sports are similarly, in part, manifestations of the physical zest of the age. Hunting and hawking must have been pastimes shared by the poor, for the innumerable technical terms used by Shakespeare would not have been tolerated by the groundlings unless they had understood and enjoyed them ; and Shakespeare himself must have acquired his familiar knowledge of these things as a poor man joining in the sports of the landed gentry. A hunt was not then a corporation or limited liability company, but each squire kept his hounds and hunted them ; and the tenants and labourers on the estate must have known them by name, as Shakespeare knew Merriman, Clowder, Silver, Belman, and Echo.

Ascham, one of the most famous scholars of his time, and the tutor of Queen Elizabeth and Lady Jane Grey, was as interested to write of archery as of Greek, and for the same reason—because he agreed with Montaigne, ' I would have the exterior demeanor or decencie, and the disposition of his person to be fashioned together with his mind : for, it is not a mind, it is not a body that we erect, but it is a man, and we must not make two parts of him '.

The fame of Sir Philip Sidney has sometimes been a stumbling-block to the casual reader, who cannot find in his writings the sufficient explanation of the extravagant admiration felt for him by his contemporaries. The truth is that they took a wider view of him than we, and admired quite as much his physical perfections as his intellectual. For we have no writer of whom a brother-poet could say as Spenser of Sidney, he was

> In wrestling nimble, and in renning swift;
> In shooting steddie, and in Swimming strong;
> Well made to strike, to throw, to leape, to lift,
> And all the sports that shepheards are emong.[1]

The queen, in this as in everything, represents her age. ' She loved ', as Aubrey wrote in his Life of Raleigh,

' to have all the servants of her Court proper men, (and as before-said Sir W. R.'s gracefull presence was no meane recommendation to him). I thinke his first preferment at Court was Captaine of her Majestie's guard. There came a countrey gentleman (or sufficient yeoman) up to towne, who had severall

---

[1] Neither, on the other hand, have we one who could write such a letter as this addressed by Sidney to his father's secretary :

' Mr. Molineaux,

Few wordes are beste. My lettres to my father have come to the eys of some; neither can I condemne any but you for it. . . . I assure yow before God, that if ever I knowe you to do so muche as reede any lettre I wryte to my father, without his commandement, or my consente, I will thruste my dagger into yow; and truste to it, for I speake it in earnest. In the meane time farewell.

By me,

PHILIPPE SIDNEY.'

Yet John Harington (*A New Discourse of A Stale Subject*, 1596) writes : ' Sir Phylip Sidney was wont to say; that next hunting, he liked hauking worst; but the faulconers and hunters would bee even with him, and say, that these bookish fellowes, such as he, could judge of no sports, but within the verg of the fair fields of Helicon, *Pindus* and *Parnassus*.'

sonns, but one an extraordinary proper handsome fellowe, whom he did hope to have preferred to be a yeoman of the guard. The father (a goodly man himselfe) comes to Sir Walter Raleigh a stranger to him, and told him that he had brought up a boy that he would desire (having many children) should be one of her majestie's guard. Quod Sir Walter Raleigh, " Had you spake for your selfe I should readily have graunted your desire, for your person deserves it, but I putt in no boyes." Said the father, " Boy come in." The son enters, about 18 or 19, but such a goodly proper young fellow, as Sir Walter Raleigh had not seen the like— he was the tallest of all the guard. Sir Walter Raleigh sweares him immediately : and ordered him to carry up the first dish at dinner, where the Queen beheld him with admiration (like Saul taller by the head and shoulders then other men) as if a beautiful young giant had stalked in with the service.'

Fuller, in the next generation, remembered that ' Such people *caeteris paribus*, and sometimes *caeteris imparibus*, were preferred by the queen '.

This regard for bodily perfection, ' the delight of the eye and the pride of life ', is strikingly revealed in the dress of the age. Rich clothes were the commonest and most acceptable of all gifts, and the most frequently mentioned in the wills of the time :

' I give to my brother Mr. William Sheney my best black gown, garded and faced with velvet and my velvet cap, also I will unto my brother Thomas Marcal my new shepe coloured gown garded with velvet and faced with cony also I give unto my son Tyble my shorte gowne faced with wolf and laid with Billements lace also I give unto my brother Cowper my other shorte gowne faced with foxe : also I give unto Thomas Walker my night gown, faced with cony and my ruddy coloured hose ' (1573).

These were the testator's best garments : a long list follows of bequests of his everyday clothes to his servants.

Men and women alike, as their portraits show, wore jewels wherever room could be found to display them—round their necks, in their ears, on their fingers and thumbs, and on their wrists and on the rosettes of their shoes. Raleigh sat for his picture in ' a white satin doublet, all embroidered with rich pearles, and a mighty rich chaine of great pearles about his neck, and the old servants have told me (says Aubrey) that the pearles were neer as big as the painted ones '.

Old-fashioned people lamented these extravagances. John Knox vainly reminded his queen that she was but ' a bonny bit of painted clay '. Stubbes protested that ' When they have all these goodly robes upon them women seem to be the smallest part of themselves, not naturall women but artificial women ; not women of flesh and blood, but rather puppits or mawmets consisting of rags and clowtes compact together '. William Harrison in his *Description of Britaine* (1587) interpolates what sounds like part of a sermon preached from his rural pulpit at Radwinter :

' Oh, how much cost is bestowed nowadays upon our bodies, and how little upon our souls ! How many suits of apparel hath the one, and how little furniture hath the other ! How long time is asked in decking up of the first, and how little space left wherein to feed the latter ! How curious, how nice also, are a number of men and women, and how hardly can the tailor please them in making it fit for their bodies ! How many times must it be sent back again to him that made it ! What chafing, what fretting, what reproachful language doth the poor workman bear away ! . . . I will say nothing of our heads, which sometimes are polled, sometimes curled, or suffered to grow at length like woman's locks, many times cut off, above or under the ears, round as by a wooden dish. Neither will I meddle with our variety of beards, of which some are shaven from the chin like those of Turks, not a few cut short like to the beard of Marquess Otto, some made round like a rubbing brush, others with a *pique de vant* (O ! fine fashion), or now and then suffered to grow long, the barbers [1] being grown to be so cunning in this behalf as the tailors.'

[1] Fynes Morison, in his account of his travels through Europe (1617), notes that ' English travelars fynde no such Barbars in any place, as they have at home ', and he complains that the barbers of the Netherlands ' wash men's beardes in dreggs of beare before they shave them with the Raysour ' instead of using ' as ours doe hott water and seete balls '.

ENTRÉE ROYALLE DE LA REINE MÈRE DV ROY TRÈS CHRÉTIEN DANS LA FILLE DE LONDRES

Pageant at the Entrance of Marie de Medici, the Mother of Henrietta Maria, into London, October 1638. From P. de la Serre, *Histoire de l'Entrée de la Reyne mère (Marie de Medici) dans La Grande Bretagne*. London, 1639

Reproduced by permission from the third volume of the *History of the Drapers' Company*

Then he proceeds to mention with Elizabethan bluntness certain less dignified parts of the body which he thinks unworthy of the cost bestowed upon them, and tells how estates are sold or impoverished to purchase rich costume; 'I have known a well-burnished gentleman that hath borne three score [oak-woods] at once in a pair of galigascins to show his strength and bravery'. Ben Jonson also in *Every Man out of his Humour* gives us a picture of a fop of the day, and says sarcastically, ' 'twere good you turned four or five hundred acres of your best land into two or three trunks of apparel'.

But money spent on fine clothes sometimes proved a good investment and was one means of attracting the notice of the queen. She was remarkable, even in that age, for her love of pageants and splendid display, and once scolded an old-fashioned courtier for appearing before her in a ' cloak of antique cut', with characteristic coarseness spitting upon the offending garment and telling its wearer that he smelt like a stableman. She also threatened the Bishop of London, who had preached in her presence against ' the vanitie of deckinge the bodie too finely', that ' shee wolde fitte him for heaven but he shoulde walke thither withoute a staffe and leave his mantle behind him'. Hentzner, a German who visited England in 1598, has left an account of Elizabeth's going to church on a Sunday at Greenwich in that year, from which we may get a picture of the ceremony she affected.

' We were admitted by an order from the lord chamberlain into the presence-chamber, hung with rich tapestry, and the floor after the English fashion strewed with hay, through which the queen commonly passes on her way to chapel : at the door stood a gentleman dressed in velvet, with a gold chain, whose office was to introduce to the queen any person of distinction, that came to wait on her : it was Sunday, when there is usually the greatest attendance of nobility. In the same hall were the archbishop of Canterbury, the bishop of London, a great number of counsellors of state, officers of the crown, and gentlemen, who waited the

QUEEN ELIZABETH
Reproduced by permission from the painting in the possession of
Viscount Dillon

D 2

queen's coming out; which she did from her own apartment, when it was time to go to prayers, attended in the following manner. First went gentlemen, barons, earls, knights of the garter, all richly dressed and bareheaded; next came the chancellor, bearing the seals in a red-silk purse, between two; one of which carried the royal sceptre, the other the sword of state, in a red scabbard, studded with golden fleurs de lis, the point upwards: next came the queen, in the sixty-fifth year of her age, as we were told, very majestic; her face oblong, fair, but wrinkled; her eyes small, yet black and pleasant; her nose a little hooked; her lips narrow; and her teeth black (a defect the English seem subject to, from their too great use of sugar); she had in her ears two pearls, with very rich drops; she wore false hair, and that red; upon her head she had a small crown, reported to be made of some of the gold of the celebrated Lunebourg table: her bosom was uncovered, as all·the English ladies have it, till they marry; and she had on a necklace of exceeding fine jewels; her hands were small, her fingers long, and her stature neither tall nor low; her air was stately, her manner of speaking mild and obliging. That day she was dressed in white silk, bordered with pearls of the size of beans, and over it a mantle of black silk, shot with silver threads; her train was very long, the end of it borne by a marchioness; instead of a chain, she had an oblong collar of gold and jewels. As she went along in all this state and magnificence, she spoke very graciously, first to one, then to another, whether foreign ministers, or those who attended for different reasons, in English, French, or Italian; for, besides being well skilled in Greek, Latin, and the languages I have mentioned, she is mistress of Spanish, Scotch, and Dutch: whoever speaks to her, it is kneeling; now and then she raises some with her hand. While we were there, W. Slawata, a Bohemian baron, had letters to present to her; and she, after pulling off her glove, gave him her right hand to kiss, sparkling with rings and jewels, a mark of particular favour: where ever she turned her face, as she was going along, every body fell down on their knees. The ladies of the court followed next to her, very handsome and well shaped, and for the most part dressed in white; she was guarded on each side by the gentlemen pensioners, fifty in number, with gilt battle-axes. In the antichapel next the hall where we were, petitions were presented to her, and she received them most graciously, which occasioned the acclamation of, Long live Queen Elizabeth ! She answered it with, I thank you, my good People.'

James, too, though he was slovenly in his own dress, loved to see splendour in his court, for we are told by Harington that ' many gallants failed in their suits for want of due observance of those matters '.

That reverence towards the sovereign as a personage almost divine which is illustrated in Hentzner's picture was deeply rooted in Tudor England. Lyly's Fidus spoke for the average Englishman when he said, ' I have learned by experience, that to reason of Kings or Princes hath ever bene much mislyked of the wise . . . Things above us, are not for us, and therfore are princes placed under the Gods, that they should not see what they do, and we under princes, that we might not enquire what they doe.' Such doctrine was heartily approved by James, who, even before he came into England, had written to his son, then aged five, ' remember God made you a little God to sit on his throne and rule over other men '. And he repeated the claim in a speech to his English Parliament : ' Kings are not only God's lieutenants upon earth, and sit upon God's throne, but even by God himself they are called Gods.' A dozen people in Shakespeare voice the same sentiments. None with more fervour than the writers of the Preface to our Bibles.

Elizabeth's only religious conviction was that a common form of worship strengthened the State by increasing a sense of unity, and of loyalty to the sovereign as its head ; she persecuted the Romanists not because she disliked their theology, but because they rated the Pope's authority above her own ; she objected to the Puritans because they opposed individual opinion to the authority of the Church of which she was the head. In the Churchwardens' Accounts and in the Parish Registers of her reign we find records of ' Fines levied upon diuers persons for not being at Church on Sondaies at Divine Service, and not shutting their windows, and selling commodities ' (St. Helen's, Abingdon) ; and of penance done by people who had been convicted of breaking the seventh commandment, like a woman whose burial is recorded in the register of Croydon in 1597 : ' Margaret Sherioux was buried 23rd June. She was enjoined to stand iij market days in the town and iij Sabeathe dayes in the church, in a white sheete, with a paper on her back and bosom, showing her sinne. . . . She stood one Saturday and one Sunday and died the nexte.'

The boldly adventurous and strongly self-assertive spirit of the age, the abundant physical energy of the people and their un-bounded zest for enjoyment, were dangerous to conventional morality ; yet if ' it was the epoch of unbelief ' it was a time when men were found ready to go cheerfully to death for their faith.

The new ideals of physical enjoyment, as well as the growing wealth of England which enabled them to be realized, are reflected in the new houses that sprang up all over the land and are still among its most distinctive charms. Harrison has a chapter on them,[1] their comforts and conveniences, their glazed windows, their costly furniture, their tapestry, fine linen, and plate,

' whereby the wealth of our country doth infinitely appear. There are old men yet dwelling in the village where I remain which have noted three things to be marvellously altered in England within their sound remembrance, and other three things too too much increased. One is the multitude of chimneys lately erected, whereas in their young days there were not above two or three, if so many, in most uplandish towns of the realm (the religious houses and manor places of their lords always excepted, and peradventure some great personages), but each one made his fire against a reredos in the hall, where he dined and dressed his meat. The second is the great (although not general) amendment of lodging ; for, said they, our fathers, yea and we ourselves also, have lain full oft

[1] He complains that ' such is the curiosity of our countrymen that not-withstanding Almighty God hath so blessed our realm in most plentiful manner with such and so many quarries . . . we take up an artificial brick in burning whereof a great part of the wood of this land is daily consumed and spent '.

upon straw pallets, on rough mats covered only with a sheet, under coverlets made of dagswain or hopharlots (I use their own terms) and a good round log under their heads instead of a bolster or pillow. . . . Pillows (said they) were thought meet only for women in childbed. . . . The third thing they tell of is the exchange of vessel as of treene [wooden] platters into pewter, and wooden spoons into silver or tin.'

The three great evils of which these ancients complained were the methods by which means were obtained to provide the new comforts : the raising of rents, the expropriation of the small-holder, and the greediness of professional moneylenders—all manifestations of the social revolution which was to end in the conversion of the feudal serf into the wage-slave and to confer upon succeeding generations the blessings of modern capitalism.

The dissolution of the monasteries, the growth of trade, and the spirit of exploration had led to a great increase in the number of inns. Fynes Morison claims for English inns as for English barbers that they were the best in the world. Harrison also praises them :

' Those townes that we call thorowfaires have great and sumptuous innes builded in them, for the receiving of such travellers and strangers as passe to and fro. The manner of harbouring wherein, is not like to that of some other countries, in which the host or good man of the house dooth challenge a lordlie authoritie over his ghests : but cleane otherwise, sith everie man may use his inne as his owne house in England, and have for his monie how great or little varietie of vittels, and what other service, himselfe shall thinke expedient to call for. Our innes are also verie well furnished with naperie, bedding, and tapisterie, especiallie with naperie : for, besides the linnen used at the tables, which is commonlie washed dailie, is such and so much as belongeth unto the estate and calling of the ghest. Ech commer is sure to lie in cleane sheets, wherein no man hath beene lodged since they came from the landresse. . . . If the traveller have an horsse, his bed dooth cost him nothing ; but if he go on foot, he is sure to paie a penie for the same : but whether he be horsseman or footman, if his chamber be once appointed, he may carie the kaie with him, as of his owne house, so long as he lodgeth there.'

Observers from foreign countries remarked also upon the prodigality of English diet: ' these Englishmen ', said a Spanish ambassador, ' have their houses made of sticks and dirt, but they fare commonly as well as the king ' ; and Englishmen travelling abroad congratulate themselves that they are better fed at home. Harrison's explanation is that ' The situation of our region, lying near unto the north, doth cause the heat of our stomachs to be

FEMALE COSTUME—GENTRY
From Hoefnagel's engraving of Nonesuch Palace, 1582

of somewhat greater force : therefore our bodies do crave a little more ample nourishment than the inhabitants of the hotter regions are accustomed withal, whose digestive force is not altogether so vehement, because their internal heat is not so strong as ours, which is kept in by the coldness of the air that from time to time (especially in winter) doth environ our bodies. It is no marvel therefore that our tables are oftentimes more plentifully garnished than those of other nations ! ' especially since ' many strange herbs [1] plants and annual fruits are daily

---

[1] E. g. that comfortable herb tobacco.

brought unto us from the Indies, Americans, Taprobane, Canary Isles and all parts of the world '. He goes on to speak of the growing luxury of the time :

' White meats, milk, butter and cheese are now reputed as food appertinent only to the inferior sort, whilst such as are more wealthy do feed upon the flesh of all kinds of cattle accustomed to be eaten, all sorts of fish taken upon our coasts and in our fresh rivers, and such diversity of wild and tame fowls as are either bred in our island or brought over unto us from other countries of the main. In number of dishes and change of meat

FEMALE COSTUME—PEASANTRY

From Hoefnagel's engraving of Nonesuch Palace, 1582

the nobility of England (whose cooks are for the most part musical-headed Frenchmen and strangers) do most exceed, sith there is no day that passeth over their heads wherein they have not only beef, mutton, veal, lamb, kid, pork, cony, capon, pig, or so many of these as the season yieldeth but also some portion of the red or fallow deer, besides great variety of fish and wild fowl, and thereto sundry other delicates wherein the sweet hand of the seafaring Portugal is not wanting : so that for a man to dine with one of them and to taste of every dish that standeth before him . . . is rather to yield unto a conspiracy with a great deal of meat for the speedy suppression of natural health than the use of a necessary mean to satisfy himself with a competent repast to sustain his body withal. . . . And among all these, the kind of meat which is obtained with most difficulty and costs, is commonly taken for the most delicate, and thereupon each guest will soonest desire to feed.   And as all estates [classes] do exceed herein, I mean for strangeness and number of costly dishes, so these forget not to use the like excess in wine. . . . Furthermore when these have had their course which nature yieldeth, sundry sorts of artificial stuff as ypocras and wormwood wine must in like manner succeed in their turns, besides stale ale and strong beer.'

We are therefore not surprised to hear that people, ' going ordinarily to dinner at eleven before noon ' ' do sit commonly till two or three of the clock at afternoon, so that with many it is hard matter to rise from the table to go to evening prayer, and return from thence come time enough for supper '—i. e. between five and six in the evening.

So nourished, as Sir Thomas Smith wrote in his *Commonwealth of England*, ' the nature of our nation is free, stout, haulty, prodigall of life and blood ' : nobly prodigal—like Sir .Richard Grenvile, whose last fight, as told by Sir Walter Raleigh, is too well known to quote ; like Drake, of whom a report made by eye-witnesses of his attack on Nombre de Dios in 1572 records that ' as he stepped forward [to take his place at the head of the storming party] his strength and sight and speech failed him, and he began to faint for want of blood, which, as then we perceived, had in a great quantity issued upon the sand, out of a wound received in his leg in the first encounter ; whereby, though he felt some pain, yet (for that he perceived divers of the company, having already gotten many good things, to be very ready to take all occasions of winding themselves out of that conceited danger) would he not have it known to any, till this his fainting against his will bewrayed it : the blood having first filled the very prints which our footsteps made, to the greater dismay of all our company, who thought it not credible that one man should be able to spare so much blood and live ' ; or like John Stubbe who could pun on the scaffold as the executioner was about to cut off his hand—' praye for me, nowe my calamitie is *at hande* ', and when it was done could lift his hat with his remaining hand and shout, ' God save the Queen '.

With the coming of James prodigality sank into grossness. Sir John Harington has left us a picture of an evening at his court in 1606 during some festivities in honour of the King of Denmark, then on a visit to his royal brother-in-law.

' The sports began each day in such manner and such sorte, as well nigh persuaded me of Mahomets paradise. We had women, and indeed wine too, of such plenty, as would have astonished each sober beholder. Our feasts were magnificent, and the two royal guests did most lovingly embrace each other at table. I think the Dane hath strangely wrought on our good English nobles ; for those, whom I could never get to taste good liquor, now follow the fashion, and wallow in beastly delights. The ladies abandon their sobriety, and are seen to roll about in intoxication. . . . One day a great feast was held, and, after dinner, the representation of Solomon his Temple and the coming of the Queen of Sheba was made, or (as I may better say) was meant to have been made, before their Majesties, by device of the Earl of Salisbury and others. But alass ! as all earthly thinges do fail to poor mortals in enjoyment, so did prove our presentment hereof. The Lady who did play the Queens part, did carry most precious gifts to both their Majesties ; but, forgetting the steppes arising to the canopy, overset her caskets into his Danish Majesties lap, and fell at his feet, tho I rather think it was in his face. Much was the hurry and confusion : cloths and napkins were at hand, to make all clean. His Majesty then got up and would dance with the Queen of Sheba ; but he fell down and humbled himself before her, and was carried to an inner chamber and laid on a bed of state ; which was not a little defiled with the presents of the Queen which had been bestowed on his garments ; such as wine, cream, jelly, beverage, cakes, spices, and other good matters. The entertainment and show went forward, and most of the presenters went backward, or fell down ; wine did so occupy their upper chambers. . . . I will now, in good sooth, declare to you, who will not blab, that the gunpowder fright is got out of all our heads, and we are going on, hereabouts, as if the devil was contriving every man should blow up himself, by wild riot, excess, and devastation of time and temperance. . . . I do often say (but not aloud) that the Danes have again conquered the Britains, for I see no man, or woman either, that can now command himself or herself.'

But the disapproval with which these excesses are recorded by all who speak of them is evidence that most Englishmen knew how to be merry and wise as well. It is time to consider the less sensuous enjoyments of Elizabethan life.

Sir Walter Raleigh, who as much as any man might have said, ' whatsoever mine eyes desired I kept not from them : I withheld not my heart from any joy ', was typical of his generation in the range of his activities ; he knew as much of military affairs, of shipping, of farming, of medicine, of statecraft, as he knew of the eighty odd wines that Harrison catalogues ; but he knew also the history of the world, and he helped to make its geography. Aubrey tells us that ' he studied most in his sea voyages, where he carried always a trunke of bookes along with him, and had nothing to divert him '.

The Homer of those Elizabethan Odysseys was Richard Hakluyt. In his book, whose title ' doth like itself heroically sound ', *The Principal Navigations, Voyages, Traffiques and Discoveries of the English Nation*, there is a paragraph in which we might fancy we heard the very voice of Drake borne down to us as he welcomes his Queen on the deck of his ship, speaking

' a word of just commendation which our nation do indeed deserve : it cannot be denied but as in all former ages they have been men full of activity, stirrers abroad, and searchers of the remote parts of the world, so in this most famous and peerless government of her most excellent Majesty, her subjects, through the special assistance of the blessing of God, in searching the most opposite corners and quarters of the world, and to speak plainly, in compassing the vast globe of the earth more than once, have excelled all the nations and people of the earth. For, which of the Kings of this land before her Majesty, had their banners ever been seen in the Caspian Sea ? which of them hath ever dealt with the Emperor of Persia, as her Majesty hath done, and obtained for her merchants large and loving privileges ? who ever saw before this regimen, an English lieger in the stately porch of the Grand Signor at Constantinople ? Who ever found English consuls and agents at Tripolis in Syria, at Aleppo, at Babylon, at Balsara, and which is more, who ever heard of Englishmen at Goa before now? What English ships did heretofore ever anchor in the mighty river of Plate? pass and repass the unpassable (in former opinion) strait of Magellan, range along the coast of Chili, Peru, and all the back side of Nova Hispania, further than any Christian ever passed, traverse the mighty breadth of the South Sea, land upon the Luzones, in despite of the enemy, enter into alliance, amity and traffic with the princes of the Moluccas, and the Isle of Java, double the famous Cape of Bona Speranza, arrive at the Isle of Santa Helena, and last of all return home most richly laden with the commodities of China, as the subjects of this now flourishing monarchy have done? '

One of the most striking contrasts in an age of incongruities is that between the bravery of the seamen and the conditions of their service. The profiteer was as rapacious and unscrupulous as ever, and, which is worse, he was often an officer of the army or navy. Sir Henry Knyvett in 1596 addressed to the Queen a treatise on *The Defence of the Realme*, in which he speaks of ' needy, riotous licentious, ingroant and base colonels, captains, lieutenants, sergeants and such like officers, who have made merchandise of their places and without regard of their duty or respect of conscience, have made porte sale of their soldiers' blood and lives to maintain their unthriftiness and disorders '. There is a contemporary picture of life aboard ship which is worse than anything in Smollett : the sailor ' must content himselfe to drinke troubled, grosse, warm and unsavourie water. . . . Such as be verie nice . . . while they shal be a drinking, with one hande they may stoppe their nose, and with the other hande lift the pott unto their head '. Food was equally unpalatable, ' lothesome to behold, hard as the divell to gnawe on, salt as broyne to feed on, and indigestible as a stone '.

But even more amazing than the enterprise of the navigators was the indomitable curiosity that drove men like Fynes Morison and Coryat to travel alone, not merely through Europe but far into the unknown beyond. In the month when Shakespeare died, Sir Thomas Roe, the ambassador, wrote from India the news of Coryat's arrival at his house :

' He came heither afoote : hath past by Constantinople, Jerusalem, Bethlem, Damascus, and (breefly) thorowgh all the Turkes territory : seene every post and pillar : observed every tombe : visited the monuments of Troy, Persia, and this kings dominions, all afoote, with most unwearied leggs ; and is now for Samarcand in Tartarya, to kisse Tamerlans tombe : from thence to Susa, and to Prester Jhac in Ethiopia, wher he will see the hill Amara, all afoote : and so foote it to Odcombe. His notes are already to great for portage : some left at Aleppo, some at Hispan—enough to make any stationer an alderman that shall but serve the printer with paper.'

To hear of the marvels of the great world which had suddenly expanded around them any Elizabethan audience, like Desdemona, ' would seriously incline ', and love the traveller, as Shakespeare loved his Moor, for the dangers he had passed. Some measure of those dangers is given in a reference in *The Tempest* to ' putters out of five for one ', an allusion to the practice, followed by Fynes Morison and other travellers, of leaving your money with a merchant on condition that he might keep it if you failed to return but must pay you fivefold if you got back again.

Yet to Elizabethan Englishmen their own country was the most interesting in the world ; and one of them tells a story, which reproaches our own generation more than his, of ' a wander-wit of Wilts rambling to Rome to gaze on antiquities, and there skrewing himself into the company of antiquarians ; they entreated him to illustrate unto them that famous monument in his country, called Stonage.[1] His answer was that he had never seen, scarce ever heard of it, whereupon they kicked him out of doors and bid him go home and see Stonage. And I wish that all such episcopal cocks as slight these admired stones and scrape for barley cornes of vanity out of foreign dunghills might be handled as he was.'

The travellers had rolled back unsuspected curtains in Space and revealed new worlds beyond them : the antiquaries and chroniclers did the same thing in Time and opened long vistas into a forgotten country of the past. The first and most zealous of those ' industrious persons ', as Bacon called them, ' who by an exact and scrupulous diligence and observation, out of monuments, names, words, proverbs, traditions, private records and evidences, fragments of stories and the like, do save and recover somewhat from the deluge of time', was John Leland, a contemporary of Shakespeare's father.

He, as he wrote to Henry VIII, in words that no preacher of patriotism has ever surpassed in eloquence,

' was totally enflammid with a love to see thoroughly al those partes of this your opulente and ample reaulme : yn so muche that al my other occupations intermitted I have so travelid yn yowr dominions booth by the se costes and the midle partes, sparing nother labor nor costes, by the space of these vi yeres paste, that there is almoste nother cape nor bay, haven, creke or peere, river or confluence of rivers, breches, waschis, lakes, meres, fenny waters, montaynes, valleis, mores, hethes, forestes, wooddes, cities, burges, castelles, principale manor placis, monasteries, and colleges, but I have seene them ; and notid yn so doing a hole world of thinges very memorable.'

Of which things he has made record

' that the olde glory of your renowmid Britaine may reflorisch thorough the worlde. . . . Now if it shaul be the pleasure of Almightty God that I may live to performe these thinges that be al ready begune and in a great forwardnes, I trust that this yowr reaulme shaul so welle be knowen, ons payntid with his

---

[1] Stonehenge.

natives coloures, that the renoume ther of shaul gyve place to the glory of no other region.'

'In thys ded Johan Leylande declare a noble kynde of stody and a naturall hart to his contrey. The Lorde of heaven send England more of suche lovers.'

In the course of his journeyings he visited the town where Shakespeare was soon to be born, and in his interesting account of it (unfortunately too long to quote) he mentions the ' praty house of brike and tymbar buildid by one Hughe Clopton, Mayor of London, wherein he lay in his lattar dayes and dyed', and wherein Shakespeare was to end his days.

In Shakespeare's own generation Leland had many successors ' enflammid ' by his inspiration : and indeed Shakespeare himself may be counted as one of them, for his tutors in English history were Holinshed (*c.* 1520–82) and Stow (1525–1605), both of whom had known Leland in their youth. These two collected, summarized, and published in the vulgar tongue the Latin chronicles in which the history of their country was recorded and which Leland had catalogued ; but Camden and Drayton carried on his work of examining and recording the antiquities of England, ' those remnants of history which have casually escaped the shipwreck of time '.

The opening of Camden's *Remaines concerning Britain* reminds us of more than one speech in Shakespeare :

' Whereas I have purposed in all this treatise to confine myself within the bounds of this Isle of Britain, it cannot be impertinent, at the very entrance, to say somewhat of Britain, which is the only subject of all that is to be said, and well known to be the most flourishing and excellent, most renowned and famous Isle of the whole world : so rich in commodities, so beautiful in situation, so resplendent in all glory, that if the most Omnipotent had fashioned the world round like a ring, as he did like a globe, it might have been most worthily the only gem therein. For the air is most temperate and wholesome, sited in the middest of the temperate zone, subject to no storms and tempests as the more Southern and Northern are. . . . For water it is walled and guarded with the ocean, most commodious for traffic to all parts of the world, and watered with pleasant, fishful and navigable rivers, which yield safe havens and roads, and furnished with shipping and sailors, that it may rightly be termed the *Lady of the Sea*.'

Yet with all their interest and pride in the greatness of their land the English of Shakespeare's day were never in danger, as sometimes we are, of forgetting the sources from which their culture was drawn : to see Italy was an ambition almost as ardent in the educated young Englishman as it had been in Erasmus ; and Shakespeare must have been familiar with many who had seen it : his knowledge of geography was no doubt gained from travellers by word of mouth. When he mocks, as he sometimes does, it is only at

> The ass that ran away to Rome,
> And was an ass when he came home.

Sir Thomas Elyot's *Governour* had the greatest influence on the education of that generation, and was the parent of Ascham's *Scholemaster*, Mulcaster's *Elementarie* and *The Training up of Children*, and other treatises on education ; its ideal of a well-educated Englishman was one who could ' use the Latin tonge as a familiar language ' ; who could read the great poets of antiquity, ' Homer, from whom as from a fountaine proceeds all eloquence and lernyng ', Virgil, whose verse ' wonderfully re-joyceth the childe that hereth hit well declared as I knowe by myne owne experience ' ; who had learned his morals from Cicero and the art of war from Caesar.

That there were many Elizabethans who could do all this is certain, for otherwise they would have been put to shame by their own sisters ; of Elizabeth herself in her youth, her tutor Roger Ascham wrote in a letter dated 4th April 1550, ' she speaks French and Italian as well as she does English ; Latin with fluency, correctness, accuracy ; Greek, even, passably well ' ; in her old age she remembered enough to cap Latin epigrams with university wits on her last visit to Oxford ; a lady of her court, Elizabeth

Hoby of Bisham, wrote Latin epitaphs on her friends and neigh-bours which may still be read in some Berkshire churches ; and her cousin Lady Jane Grey, would have been qualified to act as Professor of Greek in one of our newer universities, if Ascham's praise of her is not exaggerated. Ascham, indeed, in his *Schole-master*, assures the spirit of Cicero that ' for learning, beside the knowledge of all learned tongues and liberal sciences, even your own books, Cicero, be as well read, and your excellent eloquence is as well liked and loved and as truly followed in England at this day as it is now, or ever was, since your own time, in any place in Italy '. He disapproves of young men going to Italy to com-plete their education without proper guardianship, and quotes an Italian saying that ' an Italianate Englishman is a devil in human shape ', one who has adopted the vices of Italy and abandoned the virtues of his own country.

Against this opinion must be set the fact that the love of classical learning acted as a bond uniting the civilized parts of Europe, and almost taking the place of the common religion that they had lost ; Ascham's own correspondence affords the proof of this.

Yet it is remarkable that this enthusiasm for the classical tongues was accompanied by a great outburst of national eloquence and a new pride in English as a poetic instrument as strong as the new consciousness of England's greatness. Thomas Wilson, who died in 1581, was one of the earliest champions of the mother tongue ; in his *System of Rhetoric* he reproves those who ' counter-feit the kings English. Some far-journeyed gentlemen, at their return home, like as they love to go in foreign apparel, so they will powder their talk with over-sea language. He that cometh lately out of France will talk French English and never blush at the matter. Another chops in with English Italianated, and applieth the Italian phrase to our English speaking.' The next generation, to which Shakespeare belonged, needed no such admonition : ' Whatsoever grace any other language carrieth ', says Carew, ' in verse or prose, in tropes or metaphors, in echoes or agnominations, they may all be lively and exactly represented in ours. Will you have Plato's vein ? read Sir Thomas Smith : the Ionic ? Sir Thomas More : Cicero's ? Ascham : Varro's ? Chaucer : Demosthenes' ? Sir John Cheke. Will you read Virgil ? take the Earl of Surrey : Catullus ? Shakespeare, and Marlowe's fragment : Ovid ? Daniel : Lucan ? Spenser : Martial ? Sir John Davis and others.'

So far we have preached on but a part of our text. ' It was the age of wisdom, it was the age of foolishness.' Men who had read Lucretius still believed stoutly in witchcraft ; men who knew Socrates as a friend could none the less approve torture, burning, mutilation ; men who had learned to smile at the old astronomy believed firmly that the fate of men could be read in the stars that rose on their birth.

The good and learned Bishop Jewel exerted all his eloquence in support of the Statute against Witches passed in the very year of Shakespeare's birth, stringently enforced in Elizabeth's reign, and re-enacted with severer penalties in the first year of James I. The parish registers contain numerous entries of the burial of women done to death as reputed witches. Gipsy fortune-tellers were punished with death : [1] the burial register of St. Nicholas, Durham, has the record : ' 1592 August 8 Simsoñ, Arington, Fetherstone, Fenwick, and Lancaster, were hanged for being Egyptians.'

Yet in the Universities the possibilities of ' magic ' were by many firmly believed and assiduously explored, so that Kettel, President of Trinity, who was a scoffer, once sarcastically warned an undersized experimentalist not to conjure up his grandfather lest he should materialize as a monkey.

In these matters the age was perhaps not more credulous than our own. Only in the mildness of our penal code can we assert

[1] Though Elizabeth herself paid many visits to the astrologer, Dr. Dee, to be instructed in reading the future and in transmuting metals.

any clear superiority over our Elizabethan forefathers; their records in this respect appear to us to be brutal. Whippings, hangings, burnings, drownings, disembowellings, and mutilations were as common and apparently as attractive as bear-baiting and cock-fights. Carcasses on gibbets, traitors' heads on spikes,[1] living felons with mutilated hands and ears must have made the counterfeit horrors of *Titus Andronicus* more amusing than painful to the average playgoer. Whipping was the mildest of punishments —on shipboard it seems to have been a superstition that to avert misfortune the ship-boys should be regularly whipped whether or not they deserved it, a sacrifice to the malignant fates. Children were unmercifully beaten alike by their parents and teachers; even a girl, of royal blood, and a model child, Lady Jane Grey, was cruelly punished, as Ascham relates, for the slightest fault. Parson Harrison speaks of thrashing his children as an everyday incident—he had a dog that tried to protect them from the stripes. Youths were beaten at the universities; James I insulted the Puritan divines in 1604 by remarking that if a scholar at college had argued so weakly ' then shoulde the rodde have plyed upon the poore boyes buttokis '. Women and girls were flogged in public; beggars, for example, were whipped out of any village they might enter; and the parson sometimes recorded the fact in his parish register: ' 1610 October the 3rd day was John Hurst and Jane Wachell two poor travellers whiped.' (Askham, Westmoreland.)

It will have been observed that these pictures of Shakespeare's age show mainly the life of the well-to-do. It is much more difficult to find the mirror in which to see the common people,

> The mere uncounted folk
> Of whose life and death is none
> Report or recollection.

Harrison, who lived among them as a parish priest, shows little interest in them: they ' have neither voice nor authority in the

---

[1] Hentzner counted thirty on the gate of London Bridge, and they were a conspicuous feature in Visscher's view of it in 1616.

LONDON BRIDGE. From Visscher's View of London, 1616

commonwealth, but are to be ruled and not to rule other '. He admits that ' our husbandmen and artificers were never so excellent in their trades as at this present '—and he illustrates this by describing the skilful craftsmanship of the builders, the wealth of new fruits and vegetables grown by the gardeners, and the excellence of English cattle and sheep. He admits too, that

' the greatest part nevertheless are very poor folks, often times without all manner of occupying, sith the ground of the parish is gotten up into a few men's hands, yea sometimes into the tenure of one or two or three, whereby the rest are compelled either to be hired servants unto the other or else to beg their bread in misery from door to door. . . . Certes a great number complain of the increase of poverty, laying the cause upon God, as though he were in fault for sending such increase of people *or want of wars that should consume them.*'

Harrison makes it plain that the luxuries of the rich were gained at the expense of the poor—' the gentility commonly provide themselves sufficiently of wheat for their own tables, whilst their household and poor neighbours in some shires are forced to content themselves with rye, barley, yea and in time of dearth, many with bread made either of beans, peas or oats, or of all together and some acorns among '. The cause of this poverty is the selfishness of the merchants, ' for it is our quality when we get any commodity to use it with extremity towards our own nation, after we have once found the means [e. g. the corn laws] to shut out foreigners from the bringing in of the like '.

Stow reveals a comparison, very interesting at the present day, between the old gentry and the new landlords. He describes the munificence of great men he had known, and particularly ' the housekeeping of Edward, late Earl of Derby [*d.* 1572, of whom Camden said that ' with his death the glory of hospitality seemed to fall asleep '], is not to be forgotten, who had 220 men in check roll : his feeding aged persons twice every day, sixty and odd, besides all comers, thrice a week, appointed for his dealing

[dole] days, and every Good Friday 2,700, with meat, drink, and money '.

But the new landlords were traders and lawyers who were troubled by no theories of *noblesse oblige*. The frequent transfers of land and the affairs of the numerous trading companies that were springing into existence made the Elizabethan age a golden age for lawyers, of all people. ' All the wealth of the land doth flow unto our common lawyers,' says Harrison, ' of whom some one having practised little above 13 or 14 years is able to buy a purchase of so many one thousand pounds : which argueth that they wax rich apace, and will be richer if their clients become not the more wise and wary hereafter.' The average Elizabethan seems to have been as ready to go to law as to fall to fighting, and would have had no difficulty at all in appreciating Shakespeare's legal similes—they were a part of the familiar talk of the time, and are not peculiar to him.

The result of rural unemployment is a growing number of landless and masterless men, sturdy beggars, thieves, and highway robbers who infest the roads and make travelling unsafe so that

' no man travelleth by the way without his sword, or some such weapon, with us. . . . Seldom also are wayfaring men robbed without the consent of the chamberlain, tapster or ostler where they bait and lie, who feeling at their alighting whether their capcases or budgets be of any weight or not, by taking them down from their saddles, or otherwise see their store in drawing of their purses, do by and by give intimation to some one or other attendant daily in the yard or house, or dwelling hard by, upon such matches, whether the prey be worth the following or no. If it be for their turn then '—

Harrison describes various ways by which they accomplish their purpose :

' And these are some of the policies of such shrews or close-booted gentlemen as lie in wait for fat booties by the highways . . . when serving men and unthrifty gentlemen want money to play at the dice and cards, lewdly spending in such wise what so ever they

have wickedly gotten.'   Spending, for example, at the Boar's Head
Tavern, what they had gotten at Gadshill.

The depopulation of the villages, many of which were deserted
so that the very churches fell into ruin,[1] led to an overgrowth of
the towns and, particularly, of London.[2]   James I complained to
his parliament in 1610 that 'with time, England will onely be
London, and the whole countrey be left waste'; and he ordered
the landlords to 'depart to their own countries and houses',
there to live and keep that hospitality 'for which we were famous
above all the countreys in the world'.

They no more obeyed him than did the hungry Scots who had
followed him from his native kingdom, as the Welsh had swarmed
after the Tudors.   They stayed in London with their idle serving-
men, of whom the proverb ran, says Harrison, ' " Young serving
men, old beggars " : because service is none heritage '.   Poor but
ostentatious gentlemen like Sir Daniel Debet in *The Serving Man's
Comfort* (1598) were seen perambulating St. Paul's nave (then the
lounging-place of London) with a tail of six or seven tall, hungry
fellows in attendance.

To London drifted, too, the unemployed from the provinces,
soldiers and sailors disbanded from the wars in Ireland and the
Low Countries, refugees and outlaws from abroad, all armed with
some kind of weapon, from the primitive cudgel to the new
fangled rapier; so that the brawls of Capulets and Montagues
might easily have been described from scenes that Shakespeare
had witnessed in the London streets.   He would have heard,
perhaps seen, how Marlowe was killed in a tavern brawl; his
friend Jonson had twice killed his man in a duel, one of his
victims being a player, Gabriel Spencer.

The following letter from the Recorder of London to the Lord

---

[1] In the immediate neighbourhood of Oxford there are a dozen sites once
occupied by villages with their churches, now deserted.

[2] The population of which is estimated to have risen to a quarter of a million
by the end of James's reign.

Treasurer will help to explain why Ben suffered no serious consequences :

' Mr Nowel of the Court haith lately been here in London. He caused his man to geve a blowe unto a carrman. His man haithe stricken the carrman with the pumell of his sword and therwith haith broken his skelle and killed hym. Mr. Nowell and his man are lyke to be indicted ; wherof I am sure to be muche trobled, what with lettres and his frynds, and what by other meanes as in the verie like case heretofore I have byn even with the same man. Here are sunderie yonge gentilmen that use the Court that most commonly terme themselffs *gyntylmen.* When any of these have done any thinge amisse and are compleyned of, or arrested for debt, they then runne unto me, and no other excuse or aunswere can they make but saye, " *I am a Jyntylman, and being a Jyntylman I am not thus to be used at a slave and a colions handes* ". I know not what other parlee Mr. Nowell can pled ; but this I say, the fact is fowle. God send hym a good deliverans. I thinke in my conscience that he makethe no reckenyng of the matter.' (July 1583).

The introduction of coaches added to the congestion of the streets, which, says Fynes Morison, ' are almost stopped up with them '. Harrison gives a strangely modern picture of fashionable ladies with ' lap dogs to lie in their laps and lick their lips as they lie like young Dianas in their waggons and coaches (yea, they oft feed them of the best where the poor man's child at their doors can hardly come by the worst) '. Stow, too, speaks of the dangers of London traffic :

' The coachman rides behind the horsetails, lasheth them, and looketh not behind him ; the drayman sitteth and sleepeth on his dray, and letteth his horse lead him home. . . . Now of late years the use of coaches brought out of Germany is taken up, and made so common, as there is neither distinction of time nor difference of persons observed ; for the world runs on wheels with many whose parents were glad to go on foot.'

How order was kept among this heterogeneous and turbulent crowd by the Dogberrys who were the only police may be gathered from an extract from Dekker's *Gull's Hornbook*, mockingly advising ' How a gallant is to behave himself passing through the City at all hours of the night ; and how to pass by any watch '.

'. . . If you smell a watch (and that you may easily doe, for commonly they eate onions to keep them in sleeping, which they account a medicine against cold) ; or, if you come within danger of their browne bils, let him that is your candlestick, and holds up your torch from dropping (for to march after a linck is shoo-maker-like), let *Ignis Fatuus*, I say, being within reach of the Constables staff, aske aloud, *Sir Giles*, or *Sir Abram*, will you turne this way, or downe that streete ? It skils not, though there be none dubd in your Bunch ; the watch will winke at you, onely for the love they bear to armes and knighthood : mary, if the Centinell and his court of Guard stand strictly upon his martiall Law and cry stand, comanding you to give the word, and to shew reason why your Ghost walkes so late, do it in some Jest (for that will shew you have a desperate wit, and perhaps make him and his halbadiers afraid to lay fowle hands upon you) or, if you read a mittimus in the Constables book, counterfeit to be a Frenchman, a Dutchman, or any other nation whose country is in peace with your owne ; and you may pass the pikes ; for beeing notable to understand you, they cannot by the customes of the Citie take your examination, and so by consequence they have nothing to say to you.'

More official evidence is to be found in letters written by the Recorder of London to Lord Burleigh. In one dated 14 Jan. 1581 he reports that ' uppon Thursday at even, her Majestie in her Cooche nere Islyngton, taking of the aier, her Highnes was environed with a nosmber of Rooges. One Mr Stone, a footeman, cam in all hast to my Lord Maior, and after to me, and told us of the same. I dyd the same night send warrants owt into the seyd quarters . . . and in the mornyng I went a brood my selff, and I tooke that daye lxxiiij roogs.' He then goes on to explain how he co-operated with the Lord Mayor and the Master of the Rolls to scour London and to arrest some hundreds of rogues from Wales, Salop, Chester, Somerset, Berks, Oxford and Essex. ' And this shall suffice for Roogs.'

The crowded city was constantly swept with epidemics ; twice in Shakespeare's lifetime it was ravaged by the plague. It is hard for us to realize that the abounding vitality and buoyancy of spirit which so amazes us in the Elizabethans co-existed with a state of public health in which disease almost unchecked scourged rich and poor alike. Shakespeare, who died at 52, yet outlived most of his numerous brothers and sisters ; and a very little acquaintance with contemporary pedigrees reveals his family as typical, both in its size [1] and in the number of its premature deaths. Consumption was almost as common as it is now, small-pox, of course, far more common and fatal ; ague, now hardly known outside the tropics, was endemic in all the low-lying areas ; to be cut for the stone was what every middle-aged man might look forward to, unless, like Montaigne, he feared the disease less than the doctors. For though in Shakespeare's age the foundations of medical science were being laid, the average practitioner knew nothing of the research that was beginning, and his remedies were of the kind catalogued by Montaigne (Bk. II, Chap. 37) : ' the left foote of a tortoyze, the stale of a lizard ; the dongue of an elephant, the liver of a mole, blood drawne from under the right wing of a white pigeon . . . some rattes pounded to small powder, and such other foolish trash, which rather seeme to be magike spells or charmes than effects of any solide science '. For example, Sir Christopher Hatton sends to the Queen in time of plague ' a rynge which hath the virtue to expel infectious ayres ', to be worn on the breast ; and the Earl of Shrewsbury writes to Lord Burghley :

' I heard your Lordship was, of late, somewhat visited with the goute ; I wolde your Lordship wolde once make trial of my Oyle of Stags blud, for I am strongly persuaded of the rare and great vertu thereof. In the beginninge of this Wynter I was touched with the Goute in the joynte of my great toe, and it begun sumwhat sharpely, and yet was I spedely eased, and for

---

[1] His contemporary, Lady Temple of Stowe, had seven hundred descendants born in her lifetime.

that tyme cured by that oyle only. I know it to be a moste safe thynge. Some offence there is in the smell thereof; and yet it is wrytten of it that the very smell therof is comfortable and yeldeth streyngeth to the brayne. . . . At Handsworth this 23th of January 1593.'

> Wonderful little, when all is said,
> Wonderful little our fathers knew;
> Half their remedies killed you dead,
> Most of their teaching was quite untrue.
> ' Look at the stars when a patient is ill
> (Dirt has nothing to do with disease),
> Blister and bleed him as oft as you please.·

Yet, as in Harrison's words, ' our condemned persons do go so cheerfully to their deaths ', like Barnardine, so their high spirits were proof against all lesser evils.

For this London of mingled barbarism and culture, refinement, and brutality, pagan learning and superstitious ignorance, for this unquiet mixture of races, classes, and dialects, the plays of Shakespeare were written and staged. In the manner now following.

3
The Theatre

The corporation accounts of Stratford record that in the year 1569 the Earl of Worcester's servants visited the town and presented a play. Shakespeare was then nearly six years old, his father was the principal officer of the corporation and therefore it is not unlikely that he was taken to see the performance and stood ' betweene his father's leggs ', like another little boy, R. Willis, who about the same time was taken to see a play at Gloucester and who wrote his recollections of the event in a book called *Mount Tabor*:

' In the city of Gloucester the manner· is, as I think it is in other like corporations, that, when players of enterludes come to towne, they first attend the Mayor to enforme him what noblemans servants they are, and so to get licence for their publike playing ; and if the Mayor like the actors, or would show respect to their lord and master, he appoints them to play their first play before him-selfe and the Aldermen and Common Counsell of the City ; and that is called the Mayors play, where every one that will comes in without money, the Mayor giving the players a reward as he thinks fit to shew respect unto them.   At such a play my father tooke me with him, and made mee stand betweene his leggs as he sate upon one of the benches, where wee saw and heard very well.'

He must certainly have become familiar with such entertain-ments quite early in his youth, for the accounts record a long series of similar visits in the succeeding years.

The feudal idea that every man must have a ' lord ' who should be answerable for him was still strong ; and any company visiting a town would have to satisfy the corporation that they were not ' masterless men ', but were the retainers of some noble and had his authority to travel.   By an Act of 1572 it was provided that

' all ydle persones goinge about in any Countrey (county) of the said Realme—having not Lord or Maister . . . and all Fencers Bearewardes Comon Players in Enterludes and Minstrels, not belonging to any Baron of this Realme or towardes any other honorable Personage of greater Degree . . . which . . . shall wander abroade and have not Lycense of two Justices of the Peace at the leaste . . . wher and in what Shier they shall happen to wander . . . shalbee taken adjudged and deemed Roges Vacabondes and Sturdy Beggers.'

Many of the great fifteenth-century barons had had bands of minstrels among their enormous retinues and these had sometimes been allowed to ' go on tour ' ;[1] the statute therefore only

[1] Cf. the *Houshold Boke of Henry Percy* 5th *Earl of Northumberland* 1512, printed 1770. ' Item . . . to them of his lordship chappell and other his lordshipis servants that doith play the Play befor his lordship upon *Shrof Tewsday* at night yerely in reward xs. Item, to be pay'd for rewards to Players for Playes playd at Christynmas by Stranegeres in my house . . . xx[d] every play. Item My lorde usith and accustomyth to gyf yerely when his lordshipp is at home to every Lordis *Players* that comyth to his lordshipe betwixt Crystynmas and Candilmas xs.

enforced the ancient custom, just as the players in calling themselves 'servants' retained the old meaning of the word 'minstrel'.

The nobles regarded this privilege as a mark of their dignity, and therefore supported their troupes against any local authorities who objected to plays as immoral. The Duke of Lennox, for example, provided his company with an open letter 'to all Maiors, Justeses of peas, Shreefes etc.' who might object to their playing:

'Sir, I am geven to understand that you have forbidden the companye of players that call themselves myne the exercise of their playes; I pray you to forbear any such course against them, and seeing they have my license, to suffer them to continue the use of their playes. . . . And so I bidd you hartely farewell.'

Puritanical writers lamented the privilege. 'Alas,' said one of them (Anglo-phile Eutheo, 1580, *A 3rd Blast of Retrait from Plaies and Theaters*),

'that private affection should so raigne in the Nobilitie that to pleasure, as they thinke, their servants, and to uphold them in their vanitie, they should restraine the Magistrates from executing their office! What credite can return to the Noble to countenance his men to exercise that qualitie [1] which is not sufferable in anie Common-weale . . . by permitting their servants . . . to live at the devotion of other men, passing from countrie to countrie offering their service, which is a kind of beggerie.'

All through Shakespeare's lifetime similar attacks upon his profession gave him cause to mourn that Fortune

> did not better for my life provide
> Than public means which public manners breeds,

and to bewail his 'outcast state', disgraced in men's eyes.

Stephen Gosson in *Plays Confuted* (1579) railed at plays as

'the inventions of the devil, the offrings of Idolatrie, the pompe of worldlinges, the blossomes of vanitie, the roote of Apostacy, foode of iniquitie, ryot and adulterie, detest them. Players are masters of vice, teachers of wantonnesse, spurres to impuritie, the Sonnes of idlenesse; so longe as they live in this order, loathe them.'

---

[1] Cf. extract from Chettle, p. 16, 'that qualitie he professes'.

Stubbes in his *Anatomie of Abuses* (1583) was equally bitter :

' Awaie therefore with this so infamous an arte : for goe they never so brave, yet are they counted and taken but for beggers. And is it not true ? Live they not uppon begging of every one that comes ? Are they not taken by the Lawes of the Realme, for roagues and vacabounds ? (I speake of such as travaile the Countreis, with Plaies and Enterludes, making an occupation of it) and ought to bee so punished, if they had their deserts.'

The attacks culminated in 1635 in Prynne's *Histrio-Mastix, the Players Scourge*, of which the title-page alone is terrifying to friend and foe alike.

But until it was broken by the Great Rebellion the prestige of the great lords who threw their mantle over the different companies of actors secured them against anything more dangerous than abuse, and enabled them to tour the country as if no statute of vagabondage existed. The corporation accounts of a small town, like Abingdon for instance, show that in a single year performances were given there by the Queen's players, Master Wenman's players,[1] my Lord of Leicester's players, the Earl of Leicester's bearwards, my Lord of Shrewsbury's players, the Earl of Derby's players, and my Lord of Worcester's players. The company to which Shakespeare attached himself was under the ' most distinguished patronage ' : they had been originally the Lord Strange's men ; at his death in April 1594 they reorganized, and transferred their allegiance to Henry Carey, Baron Hunsdon, the queen's cousin and Chamberlain, so that they could style themselves ' the Lord Chamberlain's servants ' ; in 1603, on the accession of James I, they were taken over as The King's Players, ranking with the Grooms of the Chamber. The company was thus recognized as the first in the kingdom.

The Puritan objection to plays was not based entirely on moral grounds ; they were a survival from the pre-Reformation period,

---

[1] A great Oxfordshire landlord of a family enriched by the wool-trade and by a marriage with the heiress of Lord Williams of Thame.

' When the great scarlet coloured whore of Babylon . . . sette the Churche doore wide open for sundrie sportes and playes, to enter freely into the house of God '. And though many plays were now concerned with secular tales, many more still represented biblical stories, or the old folk-tales, which were associated with the ancient festivals of the ' unreformed ' church. When Gosson denounced them all as ' the offrings of Idolatry ' he was probably thinking more of the old subjects than of the new ones which were beginning to oust them in popularity ; for there is evidence that until the time of Shakespeare's appearance on the stage the religious drama persisted, at least in the provinces.

In the churchwardens' accounts at Chelmsford there is preserved a long list of garments and properties owned by the parish and used in representing religious plays ; it includes twelve gowns of various colours and materials, ten ' jyrkyns ', five prophets cappes (caps, capes or mantles ?), twenty-three beards, twenty-one hares (wigs), sheep-hooks, whips, and ' sloppes ' for devils. Various entries between the years 1563–76 show that the churchwardens received considerable sums for lending these garments on hire to other parishes—accounts elsewhere record sums both given and received for the same purpose ; the origin of these garments may be guessed at from an entry in the parish accounts of Bungay, where the incoming churchwarden for the year 1577 certifies the receipt of ' All the games players gownes and coats that were made of certayne peces of olld copes '. An earlier entry, in 1561, reveals another source from which dresses were obtained, ' Pd. at Norwich for expense when my lord of Surrey, his apparel, was borrowed for the interlude . . . xxd.'

It is even possible that the same companies of actors played in both kinds of drama ; for among the borrowers of the Chelmsford wardrobe are ' the Earl of Sussex players ', who paid ' for the hire of our garments 26*s*. 8*d*.' in 1570; the churchwardens' accounts at Tavistock record payments to two companies of players in 1562, the second of which says ' payed unto the quenes majestyse is

HISTRIO-MASTIX.

THE
PLAYERS SCOVRGE,
OR,
ACTORS TRAGÆDIE,

Divided into Two Parts.

Wherein it is largely evidenced, by divers
Arguments, by the concurring Authorities and Reso-
lutions of *sundry texts of Scripture*; of the *whole Primitive Church*, both under the *Law and Gospell*; of 55 *Synodes and
Councels*; of 71 *Fathers and Christian Writers*, before the yeare
of our Lord 1200; of above 150 *foraigne and domestique Protestant*
and Popish Authors, since; of 40 *Heathen Philosophers, Hi-
storians, Poets*; of many *Heathen*, many *Christian Nations, Repub-
liques, Emperors, Princes, Magistrates*; of sundry *Aposto-
licall, Canonicall, Imperiall Constitutions*; and of our owne
*English Statutes, Magistrates, Vniversities,
Writers, Preachers.*

*That popular Stage-playes (the very Pompes of the Divell
which we renounce in Baptisme, if we beleeve the Fathers)are sin-
full, heathenish, lewde, ungodly Spectacles, and most pernicious Cor-
ruptions*; condemned in all ages, as intolerable Mischiefes to Churches,
to Republickes, to the manners, mindes and soules of men. *And that the
Profession of Play-poets, of Stage-players*; together with the penning, acting, and
frequenting of *Stage-playes*, are *unlawfull, infamous and misbeseeming Chri-
stians*. All pretences to the contrary are here likewise fully answered; and
the unlawfulnes of acting, of beholding Academicall Enterludes,
briefly discussed; besides sundry other particulars concerning *Dancing, Dicing, Health-drinking*, &c. of
which the *Table* will informe you.

By WILLIAM PRYNNE, *an Vtter-Barrester of* Lincolnes Inne.

Cyprian, De Spectaculis lib p.244.
*Fugienda sunt ista Christianis fidelibus, ut iam frequenter diximus, tàm vana, tàm perniciosa, tàm sacrilega
Spectacula: quæ, etsi non haberent crimen, habent in se et maximam, et parum congruentē fidelibus vanitatē.*
Lactantius de Verò Cultu cap. 20.
*Vitanda ergo Spectacula omnia, non solam ne quid vitiorum pectoribus insideat, &c. sed ne cuius nos volup-
tatis consuetudo delineat, atque à Deo et à bonis operibus avertat.*
Chrysost. Hom.38.in Matth.Tom.2.Col.299.B.& Hom.8. De Pœnitentia, Tom.5. Col.750.
*Immo verò, his Theatralibus ludis eversis, non leges, sed iniquitatem evertetis, ac omnem civitatis pestem ex-
tinguetis. Etenim Theatrum, communis luxuriæ officina, publicum incontinentiæ gymnasium; cathedra pestii-
lentiæ; pessimus locus; plurimorumque morborum plena Babylonica fornax, &c.*
Augustinus De Civit. Dei, l.4.c.1.
Si tantummodo boni et honesti homines in civitate essent, nec in rebus humanis Ludi scenici esse debuissent.

LONDON,
Printed by E.A. and W.I. for Michael Sparke, and are to be sold
at the Blue Bible, in Greene Arbour, in little Old Baly. 1633.

F

players xiijs. iiijd.' ; a similar entry occurs in the church accounts at Bewdby, 1572, ' paid to the quenes plaiers in the churche' 6s. 8d. Anglo-phile Eutheo, under the heading ' Temples prophained with plaies' (1580), asserts that ' now such men [noblemen's servants] under the title of their maisters or as retainers are priviledged to roave abroad, and permitted to publish their mametree in every Temple of God, and that through England. So that now the Sanctuarie is become a plaiers stage '. Though he then proceeds to censure the writers of secular plays, his condemnation of them is more moderate : they are guilty of

' faining countries never heard of ; monsters and prodigious creatures that are not ; as of the Arimaspie, of the Grips, the Pigmeies, the Cranes, and such other notorious lies. And if they write of histories that are knowen, as the Life of Pompeïe ; the martial affaires of Caesar, and other worthies, they give them a new face, and turne them out like counterfeits to showe themselves on the stage. It was therefore aptlie applied to him, who likened the writers of our daies unto Tailors, who having sheers in their hand can alter the facion of anie thing into another forme ; and with a newe face make that seem new which is old.'

All this Shakespeare was to do.

Whether the play represented *Adam and Eve* or *Romeo and Juliet* its setting and accompaniments varied little ; it would be shown, not upon a ' stage' in the modern meaning, but upon what we should call a platform and in those days was called a scaffold ; [1] the actors would wear the costume of Englishmen of their own time—the same dress would serve for Pontius Pilate and Judge Gasgoyne ; and if the services of the Devil and his myrmidons could not be retained in the secular play, as in Marlowe's *Faustus*, a clown had to be included in the cast in order to provide the buffoonery and horseplay to which the crowd had been long accustomed and which they insistently demanded ; they had been used to a devil who would jump off the scaffold and ' make a sally

---

[1] Shakespeare calls it ' scaffolage' (*Troilus and Cressida*, I. iii. 156).

among the people ', as one of the old stage-directions ordered, and they wanted a clown or fool who, like some modern buffoons, would depart from his book to make jokes at the expense of his audience.

But while the scaffold for a religious play might be set up in the churchyard, croft, or market-place (payment for its erection in all three are recorded in contemporary churchwardens' accounts), plays representing secular tales were usually acted upon a stage set up in the yard of an inn. A few inns of that day still remain but little altered ; the New Inn at Gloucester is the most famous. The quadrangular yard resembled the quad of a small college or almshouse, being surrounded by rooms, but having an open gallery running round it, on which the doors of the chambers on the upper floor opened, for there were no inside staircases.

From the gallery the well-to-do looked down on the scaffold set up on its movable trestles, and on the crowd of poorer folk who crowded round it and filled the yard below. So the boy Shakespeare may have seen his first play from the gallery of some Stratford inn when a company of travelling players had obtained his father's leave to perform in the town.

But, then as now, London was the players' 'appointed rest, and their native country, and their own natural home'. In the pamphlet called *Ratsey's Ghost* (1605) a pretended nobleman says to the leader of a band of strolling players, 'thou hast a good presence upon a stage ; methinks thou darkenest thy merite by playing in the country. Get thee to London.' So Hamlet asks of a company, ' How chances it they travel. . . . Do they grow rusty ? ' In the early part of Elizabeth's reign the companies used the London inn-yards as ready-made theatres, with results shown in an Order of the Common Council of London in Restraint of Dramatic Exhibitions, 1574 :

' whereas heartofore sondrye greate disorders and inconvenyences have beene found to ensewe to this Cittie by the inordynate hauntynge of greate multitudes of people, speciallye youthe, to

playes, enterludes and shewes ... in greate Innes ... Now therefore
... by yt enacted that ... from henceforth no Inkeper Tavern
Keper, nor other person whatsoever within the liberties of this
Cittie shall openlye shewe, or playe, nor cause or suffer to be
openlye shewed or played with in the hous yarde or anie other
place ... anie playe enterlude comodye, tragidie, matter or shewe
which shall not be firste perused, and allowed.'

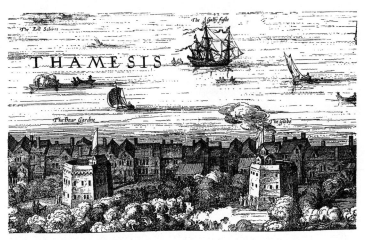

THE BEAR GARDEN and THE GLOBE THEATRE
From Visscher's View of London, 1616

A few months earlier in this same year James Burbage had been
granted a royal warrant authorizing him and four other ' servants of
the Earl of Leicester ' to perform ' Comedies Tragedies, Enterludes and Stage playes ' in London and elsewhere. The effect of
the new Order was to induce him to lease the site of the dissolved
priory of Holywell in Shoreditch, just beyond the City boundary,
and build upon it a play-house where performances might be
carried on without interference.

So in 1576 he completed and opened the first London play-
house, called appropriately *The* Theater, in which Shakespeare's
earliest plays were acted. Burbage had been a joiner, and he built

his play-house of timber, taking the inn as his model, but planning its yard as a circle, like the bear-baiting and bull-baiting rings already existing on the other side of the Thames in Southwark. This set the type for its successors, so that in later years Shakespeare was to speak of his theatre as ' this wooden O ', Jonson of ' this

thronged round', and Drayton of 'those publique circuits'. Very shortly afterwards another play-house, called The Curtain, was built in the same neighbourhood.

Several more followed before the end of the century, some by the conversion of ' Inns or common Hostelries into Playhouses ', as we learn from Stow's *Annals*. Several were built on the Bankside, a disreputable quarter, south of the Thames, among the bear-gardens and bull-baiting rings, where the interference of

THE GLOBE THEATRE
Enlarged from the Visscher view

the City fathers was not to be feared. Here in 1598 Richard and Cuthbert, sons of James Burbage, transferred the materials of The Theater, and built the famous Globe in which most of Shakespeare's plays were to be presented. As Shakespeare was then taken into partnership by the Burbages with a tenth share in the venture, he was probably one of the company who, as the ground-landlord complained, did on 28 December 1598

' ryoutouslye assemble themselves together and then and there armed themselves with dyvers and manye unlawfull and offensive weapons, as namelye, swordes, daggers, billes, axes, and such like, and soe armed, did then repayre to the sayd Theater and . . . attempted to pull downe the sayd Theater . . . and having so donc, did then alsoe in most forcible and ryotous manner take and carrye awaye from thence all the wood and timber therof unto the Bancksyde in the parishe of St. Marye Overyes and there erected a newe play-house with the sayd timber and woode.'

Our idea of the arrangements in the Elizabethan theatre is gained by piecing together odd bits of information from various sources. The most valuable of these is a collection of papers preserved at Dulwich College. They belonged to Philip Henslowe, the first Englishman to make a fortune by the stage. He began life as an apprentice in the leather trade, but by marrying his master's widow obtained some capital and speedily began to enlarge it in various ventures, including pawnbroking and the purchase of slum property as well as theatrical management. His step-daughter's marriage to Edward Alleyn, a popular actor, led him to increase his interest in the drama ; he quickly realized that there was money to be made out of it, and he built three theatres, the Rose in 1586, the Fortune in 1599, and the Hope in 1613.

THE SWAN THEATRE
From De Witt's drawing, about 1600

The contracts for these buildings are among his papers at Dulwich. As such documents are difficult for any one but an architect to understand, we give instead of the builder's contract a reconstruction of the Fortune theatre made from it by Mr. W. H. Godfrey. This agrees with drawings that have come down to us of other theatres of the age ; [1] one is a sketch illustrating a

description, written by a Dutch traveller, Johannes de Witt, of the Swan theatre, which he visited soon after it was built in 1595 ; the drawing (found in the University Library at Utrecht) was made by his friend Van Buchell, but is believed to be copied from the original. Another picture is found on the title-page of a play published in 1630, William Alabaster's *Roxana*, where actors are shown upon a stage (see above, back of frontispiece).

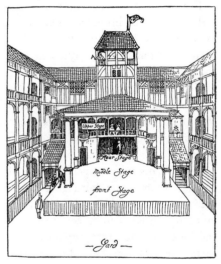

THE FORTUNE THEATRE
Mr. W. H. Godfrey's reconstruction from
the builder's contract

From these drawings and from many scattered references of the time we get our picture of a circular yard, ' the pit ',[2] open to the sky, surrounded by three tiers of galleries, and having an oblong stage [3] raised upon trestles projecting from one side almost into the middle of its area. The players therefore, like the performers in a circus, were surrounded by spectators ; and, strange as it may seem, the most coveted seats were those in the gallery *behind* the stage in

[1] Except that it is square, whereas the other theatres were circular or polygonal.　　[2] Cf. cockpit.　　[3] 43 feet wide in the Fortune contract.

a private box called ' the lords' room '. The uppermost gallery was
roofed with thatch or tiles, and the stage was also covered more or
less completely : the contracts mention ' a shadowe or cover over
the saide stage ' and ' a sufficient gutter of leade to carrie and
convey the water from the coveringe of the saide stage to fall
backwards ', so that it might not drip upon the audience.

The stage itself was sometimes a movable platform, for the
early theatre was intended to be ' a plaiehouse fitt and convenient
in all thinges, bothe for players to playe in, and for the game of
beares and bulls to be bayted in the same ' ; and therefore the
contract for the Hope prescribes ' a stage to be carried or taken
awaie, and to stand upon tressells '. There is no reason, however, to
suppose that the Globe was ever used or intended for bear-baiting,
though in many of his plays Shakespeare remembers the traditional
taste for sword-play, wrestling, and ' knock-about business '.

At the back of the stage was a screen or partition wall in which
were two doorways opening out of the actors' tiring room;
between them was a third door hidden by a curtain that formed
the background of the stage. Here a player, like Polonius or the
murderers in King John, could wait concealed ' behind the arras ' ;
and here too the prompter must have been placed. Behind the
curtain also was a recess, called in a stage direction of Greene's ' the
place behind the stage ', that could be used as an inner scene, to
represent, for example, the tomb of Juliet or the bedchamber of
Desdemona. It seems to have been immediately under the gallery,
for in Marlowe's *Jew of Malta* Barabas falls through a trap door
in the ' upper stage ', i. e. the gallery above the tiring room,
into a caldron ' discovered ' in the recess when the curtain is drawn
back. This upper stage was used to represent the battlements of a
castle wall, the upper story of a house, the balcony of Juliet's
bedroom or any scene described as ' above ' in the stage directions.
It was probably a part of the 'lords' room'. Above it was
a wooden turret from which a trumpeter announced the opening
of the play by three blasts of his instrument and from the roof of

which a flag, bearing the sign of the house, was flown to indicate that a performance was to be given.

Since the audience practically surrounded the stage, the arras or background alone could be used to indicate scenery by means of crude pictures painted on cloth; no doubt these pictures were changed with the scenes of the play. Scenery of the modern kind began in the private performances given to James I, where the audience sat, as nowadays, facing the stage. At a performance in Christ Church hall, Oxford, in 1605, when the King visited the University, ' the stage was built close to the upper end of the Hall ... and adorned with stately pillars, which pillars would turn about, by reason whereof, with the help of other painted clothes, their stage did vary three times in the acting of one tragedy '. To arrange this the college had ' hired Mr. Jones,[1] a great traveller ' who had seen plays so produced before the nobles of Italy and France. The public theatres had to wait for these accessories until after the Restoration, when, we are told in James Wright's *Historia Histrionica* (1699),

' they were introduced upon the public stage by Sir William Davenant at the Duke's old Theatre in Lincoln's Inn Fields ; but afterwards very much improved, with the addition of curious machines, by Mr. Betterton at the New Theatre in Dorset Garden —to the great expense, and continual charge of the players. This much impaired their profit over what it was before.'

Wright remarks that

' It is an argument of the worth of the Plays and Actors of the last Age, and easily inferred that they were much beyond ours in this, to consider that they could support themselves merely from their own merit, the weight of the matter, and the goodness of the action ; without scenes and machines. Whereas the present plays, with all their show, can hardly draw an audience.'

But his contemporary Mr. Pepys thought differently.

M. Jusserand has reminded us that we owe much of Shakespeare's poetry to the necessity which ' caused him to make up for

---

[1] Inigo Jones, the architect.

the deficiency of the scenery by his wonderful descriptions of landscapes, castles, and wild moors. All that poetry would have been lost had he had painted scenery at his disposal.'

But if there was little scenery in the Elizabethan theatre there was much theatrical ' property '. Henslowe's account books are full of payment for ' divers things ' bought when a new play was put on at one of his theatres : among his papers is an ' Enventory tacken of all the properties of my Lord Admeralles men the 10 of March 1598 ' ; it includes ' j caudern for the Jewe ', the caldron into which Barabas fell, ' j dragon in fostes ' i. e. Faustus, ' one rock ', ' one tome ' (tomb), one ' tree of Gowlden apelles, Tantelouse tre ', various heads of men and animals made of pasteboard or canvas painted, which may have been worn as masks or stuck upon spears, like the head of Macbeth ; Henslowe records also various payments to his carpenter and painter—' for poleyes and workmanshipp for to hange Absolome 14d ', ' unto the paynter of the propertyes for the playe of Brothers, 20s '. A contemporary pamphlet [1] refers to ' the twelve-penny Hirelings that make artificiall Lightning ' while ' Drummers make Thunder in the Tyring-house ' ; and Ben Jonson in the prologue to *Every Man in his Humour* boasts that in his play there is no

> roll'd bullet heard
> To say it thunders ; nor tempestuous drum
> Rumbles, to tell you when the storm doth come.

Shakespeare indulged the popular taste for noise and brawls by including storms, cannonades, trumpetings, and the clash of weapons in his stage directions ; but he seems to have lamented the necessity for this crude realism. He appeals to the ' gentles ' to ' piece out our imperfections with your thoughts ', ' let us on your imaginary forces work '; his contemporary William Percy, in his Faery Pastorall, goes so far as to suggest in his stage directions that ' if so be that the properties ... will not serve the turne by reason of concorse of the people on the stage, then you may omitt the sayd

---

[1] John Melton's *The Astrologaster, or the Figure-Caster*.

properties . . . and supply their places with their nuncupations [names] only in text Letters.' So in the list of ' properties ' used in his ' Cuck queanes ' he includes ' the towns of Harwich and Colchester and the Ranger's Lodge, Maldon,' which were merely painted representations of a city gate bearing the name of the town in large lettering. The ' sittie of Rome ' in Henslowe's inventory would have been similarly labelled.

In strange contrast to this simplicity the costumes of the theatre were extravagantly magnificent ; they are by far the most expensive item in Henslowe's accounts. He is constantly buying large quantities of rich material for ' our tyerman ', the costume maker whose workshop adjoined his theatre the Rose ; the ' sylckman's ' bill alone came to £14. 15. 7 in June 1601. His partner Alleyn paid £20. 10. 6 on 6 May 1591 for ' one blacke velvet cloake with sleves ymbrodered all with silver and gold ' —it will be remembered that Shakespeare a year or two later bought the largest house in Stratford for £60, that a chicken cost 3*d*., a sheep 4*s*., and a mechanic's labour for a day 8*d*. (see church-wardens' accounts of the time). Henslowe's pawnbroking business also supplied him with costumes, unredeemed pledges of spend-thrift gallants who bought expensive clothes and, as Donne wrote, ' brought them next week to the theatre to sell '.

There are many contemporary references to the rich dresses of players. The English stage plays were famous in Europe for the money spent upon them ; Coryat in his *Crudities* compares them with the Venetian drama : ' I was at one of their play houses, where I saw a comedie acted ; the house is very beggarly and base, in comparison of our stately playhouses in England. Neyther can their actors compare with ours for apparrel.' In a letter written by Sir Henry Wotton, 2 July 1613, to Sir Edmund Bacon, there is an account of the performance of *Henry VIII* at the Globe ; the play was set forth with many extraordinary circumstances of pomp and majesty including ' the knights of the order [of the Garter] with their Georges and garters, the guards with their embroidered coats '.

Yet the money so lavished was not designed, as in the modern theatre, to secure an accurate reproduction of the costume of the period in which the play was set. Shakespeare was no archaeologist; as the mediaeval artists who gave us the wall-paintings and sculpture of our churches represented Pilate's Roman soldiers in plate armour, so his Romans, in *Coriolanus* for example, carry pistols, are put in the stocks, say grace before meat and generally behave and look like the Elizabethans who watched them perform. Costume was a means of indicating rank and office more than time and place ; it was meant to reveal the characters rather than the setting of the story.

Above all, it distinguished the sex of the players ; for on the stage all the female parts were played by men and boys in women's dress. They were carefully selected and trained and must have been capable actors, for when Coryat for the first time saw women players at Venice in 1608 he was surprised to find that ' they performed it with as good a grace, action, and gesture, and whatsoever convenient for a player *as ever I saw any masculine actor* '. Many plays were performed entirely by children, particularly by the choirboys of St. Paul's and of the Chapel Royal. The petition of the Burbages, quoted in Chapter 1, explains that they had leased out the Blackfriars Theatre which their father had built in 1596, ' to one Evans that first sett up the boyes commonly called the Queene's Majesties children of the chapel '. Shakespeare makes Rosencrantz refer to them as ' an aery of children, little eyases ! ' who had drawn custom from the public theatres. Ben Jonson wrote *Cynthia's Revels* for them (1600) ; and the Induction or prologue gives us one of our best contemporary pictures of an Elizabethan audience at a play. Three children come upon the stage, and after some argument agree to imitate a man of fashion and would-be critic.

3rd Child : Now, sir, suppose I am one of your gentile auditors, that am come in (having paid my money at the doore, with much adoe) and here I take my place, and sit downe : I have my three

sorts of Tobacco in my pocket, my light by me, and thus I begin.
(At the breaches hee takes his Tobacco.) By this light, I wonder
that any man is so mad, to come to see these rascally *Tits* play here
—They doe act like so many *Wrens*, or *Pismires*—not the fifth part
of a good face amongst them all.—And then their *musick* is
abominable—able to stretch a mans eares worse than ten—pillories,
and their ditties—most lamentable things, like the pitifull fellowes
that make them—Poets. By this vapour, an' 'twere not for
Tabacco—I think—the very stench of 'hem would poison mee, I
should not dare to come in at their gates—A man were better
visit fifteen jayls—or a dozen or two of hospitals—than once
adventure to come neare them. How is 't Well ?

1st Child : Excellent ; give mee my cloak.

3rd Child : Stay ; You shall see me doe another now ; but a more
sober, or better-gather'd gallant ; that is (as it may be thought)
some friend, or well-wisher to the house : And here I enter.

1st Child : What ? upon the stage, too ?

2nd Child : Yes : and I step forth like one of the children, and
aske you, Would you have a stoole, sir.?

3rd Child : A stoole, boy ?

2nd Child : I, sir, if you'le give me six pence, I'le fetch you one.

3rd Child : For what I pray thee ? what shall I doe with it ?

2nd Child : O lord, sir ! Will you betray your ignorance so much ?
why throne your selfe in state on the stage, as other gentlemen use,
sir.

3rd Child : Away, wagge ; what, would'st thou make an im-
plement of me ? Slid, the boy takes mee for a peece of *perspective*
(I hold my life) or some silke curtain, come to hang the stage here !
sir crack, I am none of your fresh pictures, that use to beautifie the
decaied dead arras, in a publick theatre.

2nd Child : 'Tis a signe, sir, you put not that confidence in your
good clothes, and your better face, that a gentleman should doe,
sir. But I pray you, sir, let me be a suter to you, that you will
quit our stage then, and take a place, the play is instantly to
beginne.

3rd Child : Most willingly, my good wag : but I would speak with
your Authour, where's hee ?

2nd Child : Not this way, I assure you, sir ; wee are not so
officiously befriended by him, as to have his presence in the tyring-
house, to prompt us aloud, stamp at the booke-holder, sweare for

our properties, curse the poore tire-man, raile the musick out of tune, and sweat for every veniall trespasse wee commit.

Sometimes there were those 'whose hands are as hard as battle-dores with clapping' hired to lead the applause. Disapproval of a play was shown by hissing, shouting, and, above all, mewing like a cat. The theatre crowd was so turbulent and clamorous that Spenser employs it in a simile :

> All suddenly they heard a troublous noyes
> That seemed some perilous tumult to desine,
> Confused with womens cries, and shouts of boyes,
> Such as the troubled Theaters oft times annoyes.

Another picture with more detail is given us in Dekker's *Gull's Hornbook*, a satirical pamphlet giving mocking advice and instructions to a would-be gentleman. The sixth of its eight chapters explains ' How a Gallant should behave himself in a Play-house '.

' Sithence then the place is so free in entertainment, allowing a stoole as well to the Farmers sonne as to your Templer ; that your Stinkard has the selfe-same libertie to be there in his Tobacco-Fumes, which your sweet Courtier hath ; and that your Car-man and Tinker claime as strong a voice in their suffrage, and sit to give judgement on the plaies life and death, as well as the prowdest *Momus* among the tribe of *Critick* : It is fit that hee, whom the most tailors bils do make roome for, when he comes, should not be basely (like a vyoll) casd up in a corner.

Whether therefore the gatherers of the publique or private Play-house stand to receive the afternoones rent, let our Gallant (having paid it) presently advance himselfe up to the Throne of the Stage. I meane not into the Lords roome (which is now but the Stages Suburbs) ; . . . But on the very Rushes where the Commedy is to daunce, yea, and under the state of *Cambises* himselfe must our fethered *Estridge*, like a piece of Ordnance, be planted, valiantly (because impudently) beating downe the mewes and hisses of the opposed rascality.

For do but cast up a reckoning, what large cummings-in are pursd up by sitting on the Stage. First a conspicuous *Eminence* is gotten ; by which meanes, the best and most essenciall parts of a Gallant (good cloathes, a proportionable legge, white hand, the Persian lock, and a tollerable beard) are perfectly revealed. . . .

By sitting on the stage, you may . . . have a good stoole for six-pence ; at any time know what particular part any of the infants present : get your match lighted, examine the play-suits lace, and perhaps win wagers upon laying tis copper, &c. And to con-clude, whether you be a foole or a Justice of peace, a Cuckold, or a Capten, a Lord-Maiors sonne, or a dawcocke, a knave, or an under-Sheriffe ; of what stamp soever you be, currant, or counter-fet, the Stage, like time, will bring you to most perfect light and lay you open : neither are you to be hunted from thence, though the Scarcrows in the yard hoot at you, hisse at you, spit at you, yea, throw durt even in your teeth : 'tis most Gentlemanlike patience to endure all this, and to laugh at the silly Animals : but if the *Rabble*, with a full throat, crie away with the foole, you were worse then a madman to tarry by it : for the Gentleman and the foole should never sit on the Stage together.

Mary, let this observation go hand in hand with the rest ; or rather, like a country-serving-man, some five yards before them. Present not your selfe on the Stage (especially at a new play) untill the quaking prologue hath (by rubbing) got culor into his cheekes, and is ready to give the trumpets their Cue, that hees upon point to enter : for then it is time, as you were one of the *properties*, or that you dropt out of ye *Hangings*, to creepe from behind the Arras, with your *Tripos* or three-footed stoole in one hand, and a teston mounted betweene forefinger and a thumbe in the other.'

The stench of the public theatres is repeatedly mentioned, the Hope theatre, frequently used for bear-baitings, being particu-larly unsavoury, ' as dirty as Smithfield and as stinking every whit', said Jonson when his *Bartholomew Fair* was presented in it.

The gatherer was the man who took the money at the door ; Henslowe's company complained that they lost money through unnecessary and dishonest gatherers—one used to slip money down his neck under pretence of scratching his head. He took a penny for admission to the pit but varied his charge for the galleries according to the dress of the visitors, like the showman in *Bartholomew Fair* :

' An there come any gentle folks, take twopence a piece, Sharkwell.'
' I warrant you, sir, three pence an we can.'

A stool on the stage itself cost sixpence. The gatherer held a hand-bill giving an account of the play, and others were posted in the street so that a visitor might ' Read each post, view what is played to-day '. The ' third sound ' was the final blast of the trumpet which announced that the play was about to begin.[1] The Prologue, who then came forward on the stage, was the player who explained to the audience the subject of the play, asking, as in *The Merry Devil of Edmonton*,

> Your silence and attention, worthy friends,
> That your free spirits may with more pleasing sense
> Relish the life of this our active scene.

The ' Sharers ' were the owners of the building and the leading members of the company who had formed a partnership ; Shakespeare became a sharer in the Blackfriars theatre in 1608, when the Burbages, as they state in their Memorial, 1635 (page 26), ' purchased the lease . . . and placed men players which were Hemings and Condall, Shakspeare &c.' This was a ' private ' theatre where performances were held indoors by artificial light. The King's men used their public theatre during the summer and moved to the Blackfriars as the weather grew cold. The takings were divided into two parts, of which the sharers took one and paid out of it ' the ordinary repairs of the house ', retaining the remainder for themselves ; out of the other half payment was made of ' the wages to hired men and boys, musicke, lightes etc.,' the rest being shared among the actors, who complained to the Lord Chamberlain that this arrangement was unfair because of ' the extraordinary charge which the sayd actors are wholly at for apparel and poetes '. Their petition draws attention to the disproportionate amounts which ' those gaine that are both actors and housekeepers and have their shares in both '. The most prosperous of these was, of course, Alleyn, leader of the rival company — the Admiral's — whose

---

[1] 3 p.m. was the regular hour, and the performance occupied two hours, there being no scene-shifting to be done and no long waits between the acts.

endowment still supports Dulwich College, which he built on a manor that had cost him £10,000 ; but Shakespeare himself must have drawn large sums as a sharer in the two theatres with which he was connected. It has been estimated that if his profits corresponded to those of Henslowe's partners he would have received yearly £400 as a sharer in the Globe, £180 as a player, and from £6 to £10 or more for each play that he wrote. No wonder that Ratsey, in advising a strolling player to ' get thee to London ', should add, ' and when thou feelest thy purse well lined, buy thee some place or lordship [of a manor] in the country, that, growing weary of playing, thy money may there bring thee to dignitie and reputation '.

But Henslowe, whose diary of his accounts is almost our only source of information on the finances of the stage, was an exceptional man, and it is perhaps not safe to judge the financial arrangements of other companies from his.[1] His note-book records that he paid the poets Drayton, Hathaway, Munday, and Wilson £14 for both parts of the play of *Sir John Oldcastle* in 1599, with a further 10s. ' as a gefte ' when the play proved a great success. Dekker received from him in the same year about £27 for plays supplied, mainly in collaboration with Henry Chettle, Greene's literary executor. Most of it was paid in small sums in advance as ' earnest money ' and is recorded as ' lent '—

' Lent Thomas dickers and harey chettell the 2 of maye 1599 to descarge harey chettell of his a Reste [*arrest*] from Ingrome the some of twentyshellyngs in Redy money I saye lent . . . xx^s. Lent more the same time unto mr dickers in earnest of a Boocke called orestes fures . . . v^s. Lent unto mr dickers and mr chettell the 26 of maye 1599 in est of a Boocke called the tragede of Agamemnon the some of . . . xxx^s.'

Succeeding entries show that for his £27 Dekker helped to provide about ten plays during the year.

[1] For another estimate of Shakespeare's income and for detailed information on the finances of the Elizabethan stage see Alwin Thaler, *Shakspere to Sheridan*.

As each playhouse had a large repertory of dramas and gave a different piece each afternoon, individual plays were only acted a few times. In the period from 3 June 1594 to 17 May 1595, when Henslowe notes the names of the plays acted each day, there were 252 performances. Thirty-seven different plays were produced ; one, a piece called *Bellendon,* seems to have been especially popular. It was performed seventeen times during the year, and there were six performances in July ; but this was exceptional. Five plays were acted only once during the whole period. This means that the actors brought out a new play or revived an old play almost every week. Each year some plays dropped out, and new plays were produced.

The management had actors and authors alike very much at a disadvantage. Henslowe preserved, no doubt with grim amusement, a long list of 'Articles of oppression against Mr. Hinchlowe', drawn up in protest by his company in 1615. The actors complain among other things that

'Item, having the stock of Apparrell in his hands to secure his debt he sould tenn pounds worth of ould apparrell out of the same without accomptinge or abatinge for the same. . . . Alsoe hee hath taken right gould and silver lace of divers garments to his owne use without accompt to us.'

It was clearly a fixed policy with him to keep his people in his debt and so in his power. A favourite trick was to disband the company in order to tighten his hold over its members by re-engaging them on lower terms. 'The reason of his often breeking with us ', they complain, ' he gave in these words should these fellowes Come out of my debt I should have noe rule with them.'

Copies of his agreements made with various members of his company remain among his papers and show at once the failings of his actors and his methods of safeguarding himself against them. If an actor should fail to be ' ready apparrelled ' at ' three of the clocke in the afternoone ' when the play was timed to begin, he was to forfeit 3*s.* ; if late for a rehearsal, 12*d.* ; if ' overcome with drinck at the time when he ought to play', ten shillings; if unable to play at all, 20 shillings. But the worst offence of all was to wear out Henslowe's rich costumes by going to the tavern without changing them ; insurance against this danger was provided for by a fine of £40.[1]

Yet there is no doubt that the stars of the Elizabethan stage were the greatest actors who ever lived. Shakespeare himself, according to a tradition recorded by James Wright (in *Historia Histrionica*, 1699), was not among them, ' Shakespeare who, as I have heard, was a much better Poet than Player ' ; but Fynes Morison, who had seen most of the great cities of Europe, declared even our second-rate actors to be better than foreigners :

' As there be, in my opinion, more Playes in London then in all the partes of the worlde I have seen, so doe these players or Comedians excell all other in the worlde. Whereof I have seene some stragling broken Companyes that passed into Netherland and Germany, followed by the people from one towne to another ; though they understoode not their wordes, only to see theire action, yea marchants at Fayres bragged more to have seene them, then of the good marketts they made.'

Nashe, who had seen German players at Wittenberg, compares them very unfavourably with English actors.

Foreigners who visited London were equally impressed by the English theatres. De Witt in 1596 noted (in Latin) : ' There are in London four amphitheatres of conspicuous beauty ; they are named after the emblem on their signs, and they offer, each day, a varied show to the people. The two best are on the south side of the Thames and are called, after the signs overhanging them, The Rose and The Swan.' Hentzner also remarks on the attraction of the English plays : ' London possesses several theatres in which

---

[1] In Shakespeare's company things were managed differently. There was no capitalist proprietor and the company were a true ' fellowship of players ' who remained lifelong friends. And even in Henslowe's Company the selection and the production of the plays were controlled by the actors themselves.

English actors play, almost every day, comedies and tragedies before a considerable number of spectators—in magna hominum frequentia agunt . . . magno cum populi applausu finire solent.'

Perhaps the most famous player was Alleyn, remarkable alike

RICHARD BURBAGE
From the painting in the Dulwich Gallery

for his acting, so that Jonson ends a eulogy of him with the couplet

> Wear this renown ! 'Tis just that who did give
> So many poets life, by one should live ;

for his wealth, with which he endowed his college ' for a Master, a Warden, four Fellows, twelve aged poor people, and twelve poor boys ', and by which, more than by Ben Jonson's epigram, his name lives to-day ; and for his handsome person. Nashe said of him that his acting would transform a bad play into a successful drama ; and Heywood wrote of that ' inimitable actor, Mr. Alleyn ' : his greates parts were Marlowe's Faustus, Tamburlaine, and Barabas.

The greatest of Shakespeare's colleagues, ' my fellowes '. as he calls them in leaving three of them ' 26s. 8d. a peece to buy them ringes ', was Richard Burbage, whose name heads the list ' of the principall Actors in all these Playes ' in the First Folio of 1623. He played Hamlet, Othello, King Lear, and Richard III, becoming

NATHANIEL FIELD
From the painting in the Dulwich Gallery

famous for his marvellous acting of the last character ; Bishop Corbet (d. 1635) tells of an inn-keeper at Bosworth who had seen him play, and had so identified him with his part that when he showed Corbet over Bosworth Field :

> he could tell
> The inch where Richmond stood, where Richard fell ;
> Besides what of his knowledge he could say
> Hee had authentique notice from the play,
> Which I might guesse by 's mustring up the ghosts,
> And policies not incident to hosts ;
> But chiefly by that one perspicuous thing
> When he mistooke a player for a king,
> For when he would have said, King Richard dy'd
> And call'd a horse, a horse, he Burbage cry'd.

There is evidence that Shakespeare wrote many passages in the plays to suit Burbage's acting, just as he inserted an unusual number of songs in *Twelfth Night* in order to take advantage of the powers of an actor then in his company who had a fine voice; for example, he first saw Hamlet a slim young man, 'no more like my father than I to Hercules', and he may then have had in mind the lank, emaciated figure of an actor whose name has not come down to us but whose existence can be inferred from many ludicrous touches designed to make merriment of his physical peculiarities, as 'a hungry, lean-faced villain', 'a mere anatomy', 'a living dead man'; but afterwards, with Burbage's figure in mind, made him 'fat and scant of breath'.

Burbage illustrates the wonderful versatility of the men of his age; he was a painter—his own portrait done by his own hand has come down to us; and a record exists of a payment made to him for designing and making an 'impresa' or device[1] to be worn by the Earl of Rutland[2] at a tournament held at Whitehall on the King's birthday in 1613. He survived Shakespeare but three years.

Hee's gone, and with him what a world are dead.

So wrote one of his friends of his death in March 1619.

His colleague who played the comic parts, Peter in *Romeo and Juliet*, Dogberry in *Much Ado*, was William Kempe, who seems to have held that 'a playe cannot be without a clowne', and whose over-readiness to make improvised jokes, was perhaps in Shakespeare's mind when he spoke of the 'pitiful ambition in the fool that uses it'; at least Kempe broke with Shakespeare's company in 1600 and joined their rivals. His predecessor had been Tarleton, once the Queen's jester, of whom Nashe records in *Pierce Penilesse* (1592) that before he had even opened his mouth 'the people began exceedingly to laugh, when Tarleton first peept out his head', and

[1] *Vide* Puttenham's *Arte of English Poesie*, 1589, 'Of the device or embleme'.

[2] Roger Manners, who has been ludicrously suggested as the writer of Shakespeare's plays, though he paid Shakespeare 44s. to write *him* a motto for Burbage's impresa.

Meres quotes a contemporary, that 'Aristoteles suum Theodoretum laudavit quendam peritum Tragaediarum actorem, Cicero suum Roscium : nos Angli Tarletonum, in cuius voce et vultu omnes iocosi affectus, in cuius cerebroso capite lepidae facetiae habitant '. Wilson, 'our witty Wilson . . . for learning and extemporal wit without compare', Field, who had begun acting as a 'little eyass' and who was approved even by the censorious Ben Jonson, Armin, Underwood, Hemings, Philips, and Condell are only less famous.

PORTRAIT OF TARLETON
From Harleian MS. 3885

Most of these, like the leading actors to-day, were known in the provinces ; Corbet's innkeeper had probably seen Burbage act at his country town when the company went on tour, driven out of town through the closing of the London theatres in time of plague. In this way Shakespeare would enlarge his knowledge of England; we know, for example, from the corporation accounts that his company visited Dover, and there he would have seen the cliff which he makes Edgar describe so vividly to King Lear.

As we have heard from Fynes Morison, companies of English actors also travelled abroad ; his statement is confirmed by records [1] in Germany, Denmark, and France of performances

---

[1] Minutes of the City Council of Leyden, 6 January 1605 : 'The magistrates of this City of Leyden . . . have permitted the English comedians and musicians,

given at Frankfort, Elsinore, and Paris, for example, and among the players mentioned are the names of some associated with Shakespeare's company. But there is no evidence that he himself ever crossed the sea, his knowledge of which and of sailors and ships he could have gained from Dover and from the Thames below London Bridge, to which all the shipping of the world resorted.

4

The Plays

ALTHOUGH the printing-press had multiplied the number of books, the profession of authorship was not yet recognized as respectable. The 'Grub Street hack' was already in existence, and the higher members of this needy community, such as Greene, Nashe, and Dekker, served up well-spiced little pieces to attract the appetites of the populace in just the same way as the modern journalist creates a 'million sale'. So the plays of Shakespeare's boyhood, which were intended for private performance at Court, University, or Choir School, were written by schoolmasters, or by private gentlemen of literary tastes, whilst plays for the public stage were mostly put together by the actors themselves or the drudges they hired.

Later on, when Henslowe realized what marketable commodities plays were, he set people at work making them, just as he kept tailors at work making costumes—to sell them at a profit to the company acting at his theatre. His methods are well illustrated in a letter by one of his staff of hacks offering a play 'which I wil undertake shall make as good a play for y^r publiq' house as ever was playd, for which I desyre but ten pounds, and I will undertake upon the reading it your company shall giv yu 20l rather than part with it'. In another letter he assures Henslowe that he will not

according to their request, to perform and exercise and exhibit their arts in the accustomed place, namely, in the great court under the library; and this for the space of fourteen days. I VAN HOUT.'

reveal the terms of the bargain, and reminds him ' neather did I aquaint the company with any mony I had of yow '.

And, just as Henslowe kept a tireman to alter and remake costumes from stock, so he kept skilled men in his company to adapt and prepare for the stage the plays that he laid in as raw material for the purpose ; his accounts record a payment for this purpose ' unto Mr. Alleyn the 25 Septmbr 1601 to lend unto Benjemen Johnson upon his adicians in geronymo the some of xxxx s ', i. e. for adapting Kyd's play of *The Spanish Tragedy*. Shakespeare's first employment was to do the same thing for his own company ; but before this time a new class of playwrights had entered the field. They were a set of young men from the universities who saw in the growing popularity of the theatre a chance to make a living by a new profession ; the chief among them were Lyly, Greene, Nashe, Peele, Lodge, Marlowe, and Kyd ; they brought to the work both learning and genius, and their plays provided the young Shakespeare with a stimulus and a model at the very moment when he needed both. And so it happened that about 1590, just when the university wits, as they were called, had won almost a monopoly of the new profession, ' an upstart crow, beautified with their feathers ', surprised them all by challenging his masters in their own field. We can understand, if we cannot sympathize with, Greene's indignation.

The influence of the university wits, particularly of Marlowe, Lyly, Lodge, and Kyd, marks all Shakespeare's early work and helps us to date it. In ' Marlowe's mighty line ' he found the first inspiration for his own blank verse ; Lyly revealed to him the secret of ' made ' prose and the delight of playing with style ; Lodge stirred him to emulation in song-writing ; from Kyd's *Spanish Tragedy* he learned to prize the power of making the flesh creep by a representation of horrors.

A comparison between the two following extracts will illustrate the value of the new instrument invented by Marlowe and perfected by Shakespeare. The first is from an early play *Gorboduc*, written a few years before Marlowe's birth, and the second is from a speech in his *Doctor Faustus.*

> *Enter Clotyn. Mandud. Gwenard. Fergus. Eubulus.*
>
> *Clot:* Did ever age bring forth such tyrant hearts ?
> The brother hath bereft the brother's life,
> The mother, she hath dyed her cruel hands
> In blood of her own son ; and now at last
> The people, lo, forgetting truth and love,
> Contemning quite both law and loyal heart,
> Ev'n they have slain their soverign lord and Queen.
>
> *Man:* Shall this their traitrous crime unpunish'd rest ?
> Ev'n yet they cease not, carried on with rage,
> And their rebellious routs, to threaten still
> A new bloodshed unto the prince's kin,
> To slay them all and to uproot the race
> Both of the king and queen ; so are they mov'd
> With Porrex' death, wherein they falsely charge
> The guiltless king, without desert at all ;
> And traitorously have murder'd him therefore,
> And eke the queen.
>
> *Gwen:*   Shall subjects dare with force ?
> To work revenge upon their prince's fact ?
> Admit the worst that may, as sure in this
> The deed was foul, the queen to slay her son,
> Yet shall the subject seek to take the sword,
> Arise against his lord, and slay his king ?
> O wretched state, where those rebellious hearts
> Are not rent out ev'n from their living breasts,
> And with the body thrown unto the fowls,
> As carrion food, for terrour of the rest.
>
> *Ferg:* There can no punishment be thought too great
> For this so grievous crime : let speed therefore
> Be used therein, for it behoveth so.
>
>   Act V, Scene i, ll. 1–29.

Compare this with Faustus's speech when his compact with Lucifer is just about to be fulfilled :

> *(The Clocke strikes eleaven)*
>   Ah ! Faustus,
> Now hast thou but one bare hower to live

And then thou must be damnd perpetually :
Stand stil you ever mooving spheres of heaven,
That Time may cease, and midnight never come ;
Fair Natures eie, rise, rise againe, and make
Perpetuall day, or let this houre be but
A yeere, a moneth, a weeke, a naturall day
That Faustus may repent, and save his soule,
O lente, lente currite noctis equi :
The starres move stil, time runs, the clocke wil strike,
The divel wil come, and Faustus must be damnd.
O Ile leape up to my God : who pulles me downe ?
See see where Christs blood streames in the firmament.
One drop would save my soule, halfe a drop, ah my Christ.
Ah rend not my heart for naming of my Christ,
Yet wil I call on him : oh spare me *Lucifer* !—
Where is it now ? tis gone : And see where God
Stretcheth out his arme, and bends his irefull browes :
Mountaines and hilles, come, come, and fall on me,
And hide me from the heavy wrath of God !
No. no.
Then wil I headlong runne into the earth :
Earth gape ! O no, it will not harbour me : . . .
                    (*The watch strikes*)
Ah, halfe the houre is past :
Twil all be past anone :
Oh God,
If thou wilt not have mercy on my soule,
Yet for Christ's sake, whose bloud hath ransom'd me,
Impose some end to my incessant paine.
Let Faustus live in hel a thousand yeeres,
A hundred thousand, and at last be sav'd
O no end is limited to damned soules,
Why wert thou not a creature wanting soule ? . . .
But mine must live still to be plagde in hel :
Curs't be the parents that ingendred me :
No Faustus, curse thy selfe, curse *Lucifer*,
That hath deprivde thee of the ioyes of heaven.
                    The clocke striketh twelve
O it strikes, it strikes : now body turne to ayre,
Or *Lucifer* wil beare thee quicke to hel :
                    Thunder and lightning

O soule, be changde into little water drops,
And fal into the *Ocean*, nere be found :
My God, my God, looke not so fierce on me :
     Enter divels
Adders, and Serpents, let me breathe a while :
Ugly hell gape not, come not *Lucifer,*
Ile burne my bookes, *ah Mephastophilis.*
     Exeunt with him.
     (*Doctor Faustus*, ll. 1420–77.)

The next extract illustrates the style which Lyly made popular in his *Euphues,* a story or ' novel ' published in 1579–80 ; it is from Lodge's *Rosalynde* (1590), and as the story of *As You Like It* is taken from this work, should be compared with the corresponding dialogues, Act III, Sc. ii.

Trust me, swayne (quoth Rosader), but my canzon was writte in no such humor ; for mine eye and mine heart are relatives, the one drawing fancy by sight, the other enterteining her by sorrow. If thou sawest my Rosalynd, with what beauties Nature hath favoured her—with what perfection the heavens hath graced her— with what qualities the gods have endued her, then wouldst thou say, there is none so fickle that could be fleeting unto her. If she had been Aeneas Dido, had Venus and Juno both scolded him from Carthage, yet her excellence, despight of them, would have detained him at Tyre. If Phillis had been as beautious, or Ariadne as vertuous, or both as honourable and excellent as she, neither had the philbert tree sorrowed in the death of the dispairing Phillis, nor the starres been graced with Ariadne, but Demophoon and Theseus had been trustie to their paragons. I wil tel thee, swayne, if with a deep insight thou couldst pierce into the secrets of my loves, and see what deep impressions of her idea affection hath made in my heart, then wouldest thou confesse I were passing passionate, and no lesse indued with admirable patience. Why (quoth Aliena) needs there patience in love ? Or else in nothing (quoth Rosader) ; for it is a restlesse sore, that hath no ease a cankar that still frets ; a disease that taketh away all hope of sleepe. If then so many sorrowes, sodaine joyes, momentary pleasures, continuall feares, daily griefes, and nightly woes be founde in love, then is not hee to bee accounted patient that smothers these passions with silence ? Thou speakest by experience (quoth Ganimede) and therefore we hold al thy wordes for axiomes. But is love such a lingring maladie ? It is (quoth he) either extreame or meane, according to the minde of the partie that extertaines it ; for, as the weedes grow longer untoucht then the prettie floures, and the flint lyes safe in the quarry, when the emerauld is suffering the lapidaries toole so meane men are freed from Venus injuries when kings are environed with a laborinth of her cares. The whiter the lawne is, the deeper is the moale ; the more purer the chrysolite, the sooner stained ; and such as have their hearts ful of honour, have their loves ful of the greatest sorowes. But in whomsoever (quoth Rosader) hee fixeth his dart, hee never leaveth to assault him, till either hee hath wonne him to folly or fancy ; for as the moone never goes without the starre lunisequa, so a lover never goeth without the unrest of his thoughts. For proofe you shall heare another fancy of my making. Now doo, gentle forrester (quoth Ganimede) and with that he read over this sonnetto.

Turne I my lookes unto the skies,
Love with his arrows wounds mine eies ;
If so I gaze upon the ground,
Love then [in] every floure is found.
Search I the shade to flie my paine,
He meets me in the shade againe ;
Wend I to walke in secret grove,
Even there I meet with sacred love.
If so I bayne me in the spring,
Even on the brinke I heare him sing :
If so I meditate alone,
He will be partner of my mone.
If so I mourn, he weeps with me,
And where I am, there will he be.
When, as I talke of Rosalynd,
The god from coynesse waxeth kind,
And seems in self same flames to fry,
Because he loves as well as I.
Sweet Rosalynde, for pitty rue ;
For why, then Love I am more true :
He, if he speed, will quickly flie,
But in thy love I live and die.

Thomas Kyd's *Spanish Tragedy* (*c.* 1586) was the most popular play of its age, and so provided Shakespeare with a guide to the public taste and enabled him to gratify it in *Titus Andronicus,* as will be seen from the following outline of the plot:

Act I. Hieronimo is the chief counsellor of the King of Spain, whose armies have just defeated the 'Portingals' and taken prisoner Balthasar, the son of their Viceroy. After some dispute between Horatio, Hieronimo's son, and Lorenzo, the King's nephew, the prisoner is awarded to the former. Horatio, however, is in love with Lorenzo's sister, Bellimperia, and she favours him rather than the captive Balthasar. The ambassador from Portugal arrives and is entertained.

Act II. Lorenzo promises to help Balthasar in his suit. Learning from Pedringano, Bellimperia's treacherous servant, that she is secretly receiving Horatio, they manage to watch the lovers. Shortly afterwards they decoy Horatio into the orchard, hang him on a tree, stab him in the sight of Bellimperia, and leave the body to be discovered by his father Hieronimo, who not unnaturally goes mad for a time.

Act III. Bellimperia is kept in confinement by her brother, but manages to throw a letter to Hieronimo, telling him how his son has died. Meanwhile the murderers suspect that a certain Serberine knows too much; so they persuade Pedringano to murder him; at the same time they give a hint to the Watch that Pedringano may be caught in the act and also got out of the way. The plot succeeds; but there is still a danger that Pedringano may betray them, so Lorenzo shuts his mouth by promising a pardon; instead he sends him an empty box. Pedringano gaily mounts the scaffold and jokes with the hangman, who gets impatient and 'turns him off'. On the corpse a letter was found addressed to Hieronimo which reveals the whole story of Horatio's death. Affairs between Spain and Portugal are now settled and the Viceroy comes to Spain to be present at his son's wedding with Bellimperia. Hieronimo pretends occasional madness, but is to all appearances reconciled with Lorenzo.

Act IV. Hieronimo manages to see Bellimperia and they plan vengeance. As the wedding approaches, the old counsellor is asked to prepare a play for the festivities. He brings out a tragedy and gives the parts to Bellimperia, Lorenzo, Balthasar, and himself. When the tragedy is acted, Bellimperia stabs Balthasar and herself in earnest, Hieronimo kills Lorenzo. The Court are delighted at the skilful ' acting ' and do not realize what has happened until Hieronimo shows his dead son. They seize him ; but he bites out his tongue. Then he makes signs for a pen, which is brought and a penknife to mend it with ; he springs on Lorenzo's father and then kills himself.

An amusing touch, though the humour is unintentional, is given by the Induction which consists of the Ghost of a Spanish nobleman, Don Andrea, who was Bellimperia's secret lover and had been killed in the war. He appears with Revenge and together they sit and watch the play. The agitation of the Ghost as his friends suffer is almost laughable ; but he is comforted in the end and goes off to take them with him to Elysium while Revenge deals with his enemies. There are good reasons for believing that Kyd wrote a play on the Hamlet story which Shakespeare afterwards used as the foundation of his masterpiece.

The first plays in which Shakespeare had a hand were dramatized versions of ' blood and thunder ' stories or of ' merry tales ' of comic misfortunes happening to lovers ; many of these had been part of the stock in trade of the mediaeval minstrel and story-teller ; some had been printed in France and Italy and translated into English—a selection made by Painter in his *Palace of Pleasure* (1566) must certainly have been among Shakespeare's books and was used by him even so late as when he was writing *All's Well*. But the success of Marlowe's *Edward II*, and of other historical dramas by nameless authors, performed when the defeat of the Spanish Armada had enormously stimulated the national consciousness, showed Shakespeare a new means of appealing to the playgoing public, and turned his attention to a new source for stories on which to base his plays. This was Raphael Holinshed's *Chronicles of*

English History, a summary of historical records, first published in 1577, and reprinted in 1587.   From it Shakespeare learned, and taught his fellow countrymen, that, in Raleigh's great words, ' it is not the least debt we owe to History, that it hath made us acquainted with our dead ancestors, and out of the depth and darkness of the earth, delivered us their memory and fame '.

How much he depended upon the *Chronicles* for his facts will be seen from the extract which follows from Holinshed's account of Macbeth's meeting with the witches :

' It fortuned as Makbeth and Banquho journied towards Fores, where the king then laie, they went sporting by the waie togither without other companie, save onlie themselves, passing thorough the woods and fields when suddenlie in the middest of a laund, there met them three women in strange and wild apparell, resembling creatures of elder world, whome when they attentivelie beheld, woondering much at the sight, the first of them spake and said : " All haile, Makbeth, thane of Glammis ! " (for he had latelie entered into that dignitie and office by the death of his father Sinell).   The second of them said : " Haile, Makbeth, thane of Cawder ! "   But the third said :   " All haile, Makbeth, that heereafter shalt be king of Scotland ! "

Then Banquho: "What manner of women " (saith he) "are you, that seeme so little favorable unto me, whereas to my fellow heere, besides high offices, ye assigne also the kingdom, appointing foorth for me nothing at all ? "   " Yes " (saith the first of them) " we promise greater benefits unto thee, than unto him, for he shall reigne in deed, but with an unluckie end ; neither shall he leave anie issue behind to succeed in his place, where contrarilie thou in deed shalt not reigne at all, but of thee those shall be borne which shall governe the Scotish kingdome by long order of continuall descent."   Herewith the foresaid women vanished immediatlie out of their sight.   This was reputed at the first but some vaine fantasticall illusion by Mackbeth and Banquho, insomuch that Banquho would call Mackbeth in jest, King of Scotland ; and Mackbeth againe would call him in sport likewise, the father of manie kings.   But afterwards the common opinion was, that these women were either the weird sisters, that is (as ye would say) the goddesses of destinie, or else some nymphs or feiries, indued with knowledge of prophesie by their necromanticall science, bicause everie thing came to pass as they had spoken. For shortlie after, the thane of Cawder being condemned at Fores of treason against the king committed ; his lands, livings, and offices were given of the kings liberalitie to Mackbeth '. . . .

(For a time Macbeth thought that he would succeed to the kingdom, but Duncan appointed one of his sons as his heir. This was considered a grievance by Macbeth.)

' The woords of the three weird sisters also (of whom before ye have heard) greatlie incouraged him hereunto, but speciallie his wife lay sore upon him to attempt the thing, as she that was verie ambitious, burning in unquenchable desire to beare the name of a queene. At length therefore, communicating his purposed intent with his trustie friends, amongst whome Banquho was the chiefest, upon confidence of their promised aid, he slue the king at Enverns, or (as some say) at Botgosvane, in the sixt yeare of his reigne.'

As this account of Macbeth's crime was not suitable to Shakespeare's purpose, he turned to the story of the murder of Duff by Donwald, who also was driven on by his wife.

' Donwald thus being the more kindled in wrath by the words of his wife, determined to follow hir advise in the execution of so heinous an act. Wherupon devising with himselfe for a while which way hee might best accomplish his cursed intent, at length gat opportunitie, and sped his purpose as followeth. It chanced that the king upon the daie before he purposed to depart foorth of the castell, was long in his oratorie at his praiers, and there continued till it was late in the night. At last, comming foorth, he called such afore him as had faithfullie served him in the pursute and apprehension of the rebels and giving them heartie thanks, he bestowed sundrie honourable gifts amongst them, of the which number Donwald was one, as he that had beene ever accounted a most faithfull servant to the king.

At length, having talked with them a long time he got him into his privie chamber, onelie with two of his chamberlains, who having brought him to bed, came foorth againe, and then fell to banketting with Donwald and his wife, who had prepared diverse delicate dishes, and sundrie sorts of drinks for their reare supper or collation, wherat they sate up so long, till they had charged their stomachs with such full gorges, that their heads were no sooner got to the pillow, but asleepe they were so fast that a man might have remooved the chamber over them, sooner than to have awaked them out of their droonken sleepe.'

(Donwald then sends four of his servants in to murder the king. The corpse is taken away and hidden at the bottom of a stream.)

' Donwald, about the time that the murther was in dooing, got him amongst them that kept watch, and so continued in companie with them all the residue of the night. But in the morning when the noise was raised in the kings chamber how the king was slaine, his bodie conveied awaie, and the bed all beraied with bloud ; he with the watch ran thither, as though he had knowne nothing of the matter, and breaking into the chamber, and finding cakes of bloud in the bed, and on the floore about the sides of it, he foorth-with slue the chamberleins, as guiltie of that heinous murther, and then like a mad man running to and fro, he ransacked everie corner within the castell, as though it had beene to have seene if he might have found either the bodie or anie of the murtherers hid in anie privie place : but at length comming to the posterne gate, and finding it open, he burdened the chamberleins, whome he had slaine, with all the fault, they having the keies of the gates committed to their keeping all the night, and therefore it could not be otherwise (said he) but that they were of counsell in committing of that detestable murther.'

From dramatizing stories of British history Shakespeare passed on, about the turn of the century, to re-create on the stage some of the great figures of antiquity. But whereas in Holinshed he had found merely a mine of facts from which he had selected some, rejected some, and altered some as he thought best for his purpose, the book which now inspired him was one which not even he could improve upon. In his youth he had learnt from Marlowe, and passed beyond him ; in his maturity he could do no more than show great men to his own age as Plutarch had shown them to his.[1]

Plutarch's *Lives of the noble Grecians and Romanes* had been translated from the original Greek into French by Jacques Amyot

---

[1] Shakespeare's knowledge of women was however more profound even than Plutarch's. See pp. 116–19.

in 1559, and from the French into English by Sir Thomas North in 1579. It is unlikely that Shakespeare became acquainted with the book until it was reprinted in a second edition in 1595.

It will be seen from the extracts which follow that Shakespeare owed almost as much to the marvellous prose of Sir Thomas North as to the genius for character-drawing of Plutarch ; in the whole history of literature no great book except perhaps the Bible has been so greatly translated. His treatment of his material reveals Shakespeare as a critic of the first order : he realized the perfection of the form and he left it untouched, merely grouping North's phrases into the pattern of his blank verse.

Volumnia's Speech : Life of Coriolanus (cf. Shakespeare's
Coriolanus, V. iii. 94–125).

' Then she spake in this sort : " If we held our peace, my son, and determined not to speak, the state of our poor bodies and present sight of our raiment, would easily bewray to thee what life we have led at home, since thy exile and abode abroad ; but think now with thyself, how much more unfortunate than all the women living, we are come hither, considering that the sight which should be most pleasant to all other to behold, spiteful fortune had made most fearful to us : making myself to see my son and my daughter her husband besieging the walls of his native country so as that which is the only comfort to all other in their adversity and misery, to pray unto the gods and to call to them for aid, is the only thing which plungeth us into most deep perplexity. For we cannot alas together pray both for victory to our country and for safety to thy life also: but a world of grievous curses, yea, more than any mortal enemy can heap upon us, are forcibly wrapt up in our prayers. For the bitter sop of most hard choice is offered thy wife and children, to forgo one of the two ; either to lose the person of thyself, or the nurse of their native country. For myself, my son, I am determined not to tarry till fortune, in my lifetime, do make an end of this war. For if I cannot persuade thee, rather to do good unto both parties than to overthrow and destroy the one, preferring love and nature before the malice and calamity of wars, thou shalt see, my son, and trust unto it, thou shalt no sooner march forward to assault thy country, but thy foot shall tread upon thy mother's womb, that brought thee first into this world. And I may not defer to see the day either that my son be led prisoner in triumph by his natural countrymen or that he himself do triumph of them and of his natural country. For if it were so, that my request tended to save my country in destroying the Volsces, I must confess, thou wouldest hardly and doubtfully resolve on that. For as, to destroy thy natural country, it is altogether unmeet and unlawful, so were it not just, and less honourable, to betray those that put their trust in thee. But my only demand consisteth, to make a gaol-delivery of all evils, which delivereth equal benefit and safety both to the one and to the other, but most honourable for the Volsces. For it shall appear, that, having victory in their hands, they have of special favour granted us singular graces, peace, and amity, albeit themselves have no less part of both than we. Of which good, if so it come to pass, thyself is the only author, and so hast thou the only honour. But if it fail and fall out contrary, thyself alone deservedly shalt carry the shameful reproach and burden of either party. So, though the end of war be uncertain, yet this notwithstanding is most certain, that, if it be thy chance to conquer, this benefit shalt thou reap of thy goodly conquest, to be chronicled the plague and destroyer of thy country. And if fortune overthrow thee, then the world will say that, through desire to revenge thy private injuries thou hast for ever undone thy good friends who did most lovingly and courteously receive thee.'

Plutarch was fascinated by the play and clash of character in great men's lives and not by the mere fact of biography, for he had a fine dramatic sense, and his vivid pictures of men and events were invaluable to a dramatist. The death of Cleopatra (*Antony and Cleopatra*, Act V, sc. ii.) almost exactly reproduces Plutarch's description in the Life of Antony.

' Shortly after, Caesar came himself in person to see her, and to comfort her, Cleopatra, being laid upon a little low bed in poor estate (when she saw Caesar come into her chamber), suddenly rose up, naked in her smock, and fell down at his feet marvellously disfigured : both for that she had plucked her hair from her head, as also for that she had martyred all her face with her nails ; and besides, her voice was small and trembling, her eyes sunk into her head with continual blubbering ; and moreover, they might see the most part of her stomach torn in sunder. To be short, her body was not much better than her mind ; yet her good grace and comelinesses and the force of her beauty was not altogether defaced. But notwithstanding this ugly and pitiful state of hers, yet she shewed herself within, by her outward looks and countenance. When Caesar had made her lie down again, and sat by her bedside, Cleopatra began to clear and excuse herself for that she had done, laying all to the fear she had of Antonius : Caesar, in contrary manner, reproved her in every point. Then she suddenly altered her speech, and prayed him to pardon her, as though she were afraid to die, and desirous to live. At length, she gave him a brief and memorial of all the ready money and treasure she had. But by chance there stood one Seleucus by, one of her treasurers, who, to seem a good servant, came straight to Caesar to disprove Cleopatra, that she had not set in all, but kept many things back of purpose. Cleopatra was in such a rage with him, that she flew upon him, and took him by the hair of the head, and boxed him well-favouredly. Caesar fell a laughing and parted the fray. "Alas," said she, "O Caesar : is not this a great shame and reproach, that thou having vouchsafed to take the pains to come unto me, and done me this honour, poor wretch and catiff creature, brought into this pitiful and miserable state : and that mine own servants should come now to accuse me ? though it may be I have reserved some jewels and trifles meet for women, but not for me (poor soul) to set out myself withal, but meaning to give some pretty presents and gifts unto Octavia and Livia, that they, making means and intercessions for me to thee, thou mightest yet extend thy favour and mercy upon me." Caesar was glad to hear her say so, persuading himself thereby that she had yet a desire to save her life. So he made her answer, that he did not only give her that to dispose of at her pleasure which she had kept back, but further promised to use her more honourably and bountifully than she would think for : and so he took his leave of her, supposing he had deceived her, but indeed he was deceived himself. There was a young gentleman, Cornelius Dolabella, that was one of Caesar's very great familiars, and besides did bear no ill will unto Cleopatra. He sent her word secretly (as she had requested him) that Caesar determined to take his journey through Syria, and that within three days he would send her away before with her children. When this was told Cleopatra, she requested Caesar that it would please him to suffer her to offer the last oblations of the dead unto the soul of Antonius. This being granted her, she was carried to the place where the tomb was, and there falling down on her knees, embracing the tomb with her women, the tears running down her cheeks, she began to speak in this sort : " O my dear Lord Antonius, it is not long sithence I buried thee here, being a free woman : and now I offer unto thee the funeral sprinklings and oblations, being a captive and prisoner ; and yet I am forbidden and kept from tearing and murdering this captive body of mine with blows, which they carefully guard and keep only to triumph of thee : look therefore henceforth for no other honours, offerings, nor sacrifices from me : for these are the last which Cleopatra can give thee, sith now they carry her away. Whilst we lived together, nothing could sever our companies : but now at our death, I fear me they will make us change our countrie. For as thou, being a Roman, hast been buried in Egypt : even so, wretched creature, I, an Egyptian, shall be buried in Italy, which shall be all the good I shall have received by thy country. If therefore the gods where thou art now have any power and authority, sith our gods here have forsaken us, suffer not thy true friend and lover to be carried away alive, that in me they triumph in thee ; but receive me with thee, and let me be buried in one self tomb with thee. For though my griefs and miseries be infinite, yet none have greived me more, nor that I could bear less withal, than this small time which I have been driven to live alone without thee."

Then having ended these doleful plaints, and crowned the tomb with garlands and sundry nosegays, and marvellous lovingly embraced the same, she commanded they should prepare her bath ; and when she had bathed and washed herself, she fell to her meat, and was sumptuously served. Now whilst she was at dinner, there came a countryman and brought her a basket. The soldiers that warded at the gates, asked him straight what he had in his basket. He opened his basket, and took out the leaves that covered the figs, and showed them that they were figs he brought. They all of them marvelled to see so goodly figs. The countryman laughed to hear them, and bade them to take some if they would. They believed he told them truly, and so bade him carry them in. After Cleopatra had dined, she sent a certain table written and sealed unto Caesar, and commanded them all to go out of the tombs where she was, but the two women ; then she shut the doors to her. Caesar, when he had received this table, and began to read her lamentation and petition, requesting him that he would let her be buried with Antonius, found straight what she meant, and thought to have gone thither himself : howbeit, he sent one before in all haste that might be, to see what it was. Her death was very sudden : for those whom Caesar sent unto her ran thither with all haste possible, and found the soldiers standing at the gate, mistrusting nothing, nor understanding of her death. But when they had opened the doors, they found Cleopatra stark-dead, laid upon a bed of gold, attired and arrayed in her royal robes, and one of her two women, which was called Iras, dead at her feet : her other woman (called Charmion) half dead, and trembling, trimming the diadem which Cleopatra wore upon her head. One of the soldiers seeing her, angrily said unto her : " Is this well done, Charmion ? " "Very well," said she again, " and meet for a princess descended from the race of so many kings " ; she said no more, but fell down dead hard by the bed.'

The books thus used as quarries Shakespeare must have owned and kept by him in his room in Silver Street. There is a passage in *The Tempest* which proves that he had read Montaigne's essay ' Of Cannibals ' ; there are several allusions that show he had read Arthur Golding's translations of Ovid, with whom he may have made some acquaintance at school ; he probably had a copy of the Genevan Bible, and heard the Bishops' version read when he went to church. But there is no evidence that he ever owned a store of books, or even that he was interested in books except as tools or raw material ; and there is plenty of evidence that the man who could appreciate Plutarch to the point of reverence could read with zest the popular books of riddles, merry tales, jests, ' wits, fits and fancies ' which provided the Elizabethan populace with merriment. If the scraps of old songs and ballads, the allusions to current jests, the tags from popular romances, plays, and chap-books, the proverbs and catch-words of the age, could be all identified and collected, it would probably be found that in mere bulk they far exceeded all that Shakespeare had borrowed from any other source. His dialogue, as Dr. Johnson said, ' seems to have been gleaned by diligent selection out of common conversation '.

And even when he went to books, as he did for most of his plots, ' he chose the most popular, such as were read by many, and related by more ; for his audience could not have followed through the intricacies of the drama, had they not held the thread of the story in their hands '.　Johnson adds the reminder, still more necessary to-day, that ' the stories, which we now find only in remoter authours, were in his time accessible and familiar ' ; and he gives a warning, which many later critics have not heeded, that the literature favoured by Shakespeare was not ' Chaucer or Saxo Grammaticus ' but popular versions told by word of mouth or printed in cheap pamphlets now long forgotten.

He shared with the groundlings in his audience a liking for ' topical allusions '.　Most of them, of course, are lost on us to-day, but some are still obvious and enable us approximately to date the plays in which they occur.　Thus a reference in *Macbeth* to kings

> That two-fold balls and treble sceptres carry

suggests the accession of James I as the period when the play was written ; and in the chorus in the last act of *Henry V* the lines

> Were now the general of our gracious empress,
> (As in good time he may) from Ireland coming,
> Bringing rebellion brooched on his sword,

obviously refer to the Earl of Essex, who was sent to Ireland in April 1599 and returned in September ; while the ' wooden O ' in the Prologue may be the Globe theatre, newly built in the same year.　Mention in *Lear* of ' late eclipses in the sun and moon ' followed by ' Machinations, hollowness, treachery and all ruinous disorders ', suggests the autumn of 1605, when eclipses of the moon and sun were followed by the discovery of the Gunpowder Plot. And the earthquake that is mentioned by the nurse to fix Juliet's age may be the great earthquake of April 1580.

The exact dates of the plays and the order in which they were written are problems that admit only approximate solutions. When an author had finished his work he sold his manuscript to the players' company, who henceforth considered it as much their property as the stock costumes. They would not be disposed to print it, for people might be content to read it instead of coming to see it played, or it might be put on the stage by a rival company. But there was also the risk that a play found to be popular might be stolen and printed by a ' pirate '; shorthand writers were sometimes employed for this purpose, or hangers-on at the theatre were bribed to repeat what they could learn by heart. In this way five of Shakespeare's plays were printed from ' diverse stolne and surreptitious copies, maimed, and deformed by the frauds and stealthes of injurious imposters, that expos'd them '.

All printing was controlled by the Stationers' Company or gild ; and no book might be published unless the printer had first obtained a licence from the Archbishop of Canterbury's officials and entered the title in the Stationer's Register. This might be done as well by a pirate as by the rightful owners of a play, and it was probably to forestall a piracy that Shakespeare's Company in 1600 entered some of their stock of plays on the Stationers' Register. The Entry records

                my lord chamberlens menns plaies Entred
          27 may 1600   viz
    to master Robertes   *A moral of clothe breeches and velvet hose*
    27 May to hym   *Allarum to London*
                            4 Augusti
            As you like yt a booke
            Henry the Fift a booke   to be
            Every Man in his humour a booke   staied
            The comedie of *much adoo about nothing* a booke

The words ' to be staied ' meant that the manuscripts were not to be printed until they had been licensed. They then sold *Much Ado,* which was properly licensed on 14th August : *Henry V* had already been ' stolne ' : *As You Like It* did not appear until the First Folio.

When times were bad a company might itself raise money by selling manuscripts to the printer ; forty shillings seems to have been the usual price for a play. Thus in 1593-4, when there was an outbreak of plague, and in 1600–1, when the theatres were suffering from Puritanism, many plays were printed. Fourteen of Shakespeare's were quite regularly published in quarto form during his lifetime.

The date of entry or of publication proves that a play was then in existence, but does not tell how long it had been written. So it is with other contemporary notices ; we learn from Meres (see page 21) that twelve of Shakespeare's plays had been written before 1598. The diary kept by John Manningham, a barrister of the Middle Temple, is in the British Museum ; an entry under the date 2nd February 1601 [–2] notes :

' At our feast, wee had a play called Twelve Night, or What You Will, much like the Commedy of Errors, or Menechmi in Plautus, but most like and neere to that in Italian called Inganni [The Cheats]. A good practise in it to make the steward beleeve his lady widowe was in love with him, by counterfayting a letter as from his lady in generall termes, telling him what shee liked best in him, and prescribing his gesture in smiling, his apparaile &c., and then when he came to practise making him believe they took him to be mad &c.'

John Weever's *Mirror of Martyrs*, published in 1601, contains a stanza clearly referring to *Julius Caesar* :

> The many-headed multitude were drawne
> By *Brutus* speech that *Caesar* was ambitious,
> When eloquent *Mark Antonie* had showne
> His vertues, who but *Brutus* then was vicious ?

A certain Dr. Forman, who seems to have been a keen play-goer, made some notes on plays he had seen ; his manuscript, which he called ' The Bocke of Plaies and Notes thereof per Formans for common pollicie ', is now in the Bodleian Library. He gives an outline of the plot ' In Mackbeth at the glob, 1610, the 20 of Aprill, Saturday ' ; he noted ' In the Winters Talle at the Glob, 1611, the 15 of maye how he sent to the orakell of Appollo ' and ' also the Rog that cam in all tottered like roll papri '[1] ; at the same time he

---

[1] Tattered like a roll of paper.

wrote a sketch of ' Cimbalin, King of England ' but unfortunately omits to mention the date of the performance.   However, it must have been in one or other of these two years, 1610–11.

Records of payment for a performance at court, some of which have been quoted (page 21), also give clues to the dates of certain plays ; but all this merely allows us to group the plays as ' early ', ' middle ' or ' late '.

Attempts have been made to establish the order of the plays by the study of the gradual change in Shakespeare's style.   In the plays shown by the records to be ' early ' there is a frequent use of rhyme, while in the last group rhyme is abandoned.   The percentage of rhyming lines may therefore give a key to the order. Similarly in the early plays most of the lines are ' end-stopped ', i. e. the stress at the end of the line coincides with the end of the sentence.   In *Love's Labour's Lost,* written about 1592, for example a typical passage is

Biron : Well, say I am ; why should proud summer boast
Before the birds have any cause to sing ?
Why should I joy in any abortive birth ?
At Christmas I no more desire a rose
Than wish a snow in May's new-fangled shows ;
But like of each thing that in season grows.
So you, to study now it is too late,
That were to climb o'er the house to unlock the gate.
(I. i. 101.)

In the latest plays end-stopped lines are rare, as a speech from *The Tempest* will show :
But this rough magic
I here abjure ; and when I have required
Some heavenly music (which even now I do)
To work mine end upon their senses, that
This airy charm is for, I'll break my staff,
Bury it certain fathoms in the earth,
And, deeper than did ever plummet sound,
I'll drown my book.   (V. i. 50.)

Here, again, scales have been made by men of leisure showing the proportion of ' end-stopped ' and ' run-on ' lines in each play ; thus it has been calculated that in *Love's Labour's Lost* the ' run-on ' lines are as 1 to 18, while in *The Winter's Tale* they are as 1 to 2.

Though very few manuscripts of Elizabethan plays have come down to us, enough remains to enable scholars to trace the stages in the life of a play from the time when it lay finished on Shakespeare's table until we read it in a twentieth-century edition.

As soon as the complete play was handed over to the company the parts of the different actors were copied out and marked with their ' cues ' ; the prompter then went over each part and added his notes of ' business ', alarums and the like. The parts were now ready for distribution among the actors—the manuscript of Alleyn's actual part for *Orlando Furioso* (a play of Greene's) may still be seen at Dulwich ; it was originally fastened in a roll for convenient holding at rehearsals. But before rehearsals could begin the manuscript had to be sent to the Queen's Master of the Revels to be licensed for performance, for an Act of 1 Elizabeth forbade ' al maner Interludes to be playde, eyther openly or privately, except the same be notified before hand and licensed ', which they are not to be if in them ' either matters of religion or of the governaunce of the estate shalbe handled '. This licence cost 7s. and was really a safeguard both to the State and the actors, for the officials censored, according to law, passages in which ' either matters of religion or of the governaunce of the estate ' were ' handled ', and thereby freed the players from the risk of prosecution.

In the British Museum there is a manuscript [1] of the greater part of a play called *The Book of Sir Thomas More*, in which, as sheriff of London, More is shown quieting a riot by the London mob. Most of it is in the handwriting of the playwright Anthony Munday ; but at the top of his first page is written ' Leave out ye insurrection wholy and the cause thereoff, and begin with Sir Tho. Moore at ye mayors sessions, with a reportt

---

[1] (Harleian, 7368).

afterwards off his good service don, being shrive off London, uppon a mutiny agaynst ye Lumbardes, only by a shortt reportt, and nott otherwise, att your own perrilles. E. Tyllney.' In the margins of other pages are more notes in the same hand, as 'Mend yt' or 'This must be newe written'. And a great part of the play has in consequence been 'newe written'; for Sir Edmund Tilney was Elizabeth's Master of the Revels and licenser of plays (from 1579 to her death). There were riots in

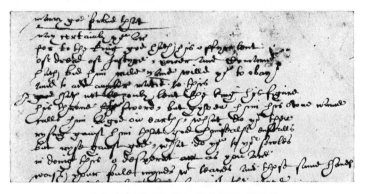

THE BOOK OF SIR THOMAS MORE
Handwriting believed to be Shakespeare's

London in 1586 and 1595, and this play was probably sent to Tilney in the latter year. The alterations, on sheets of paper of several sorts and sizes pasted above the original leaves or inserted among them, are in four or five different hands, as if the manager, anxious to get his play on the stage with the least possible delay, had divided the work of revision among several writers.

One of these is believed to be Shakespeare himself. The three pages of manuscript substituted for the scene that had offended the censor include passages worthy of Shakespeare at his best, and they are written in a hand that agrees with the six signatures which are the only other specimens of his writing that have come down to us.

The methods of the printing-house in Shakespeare's day help to explain why so few manuscripts have survived. Proofs were rarely sent out ; and when Heming and Condell sent Shakespeare's copy to the press in 1623 they probably saw the sheets at the printers' before they were printed off, and therefore did not trouble to take away the manuscript.

The Folio is neither beautifully printed nor consistently compiled. Except for the divisions into Comedies, Histories, and Tragedies, there is no attempt at order, nor are the plays themselves carefully edited. Where the play had already been published the Quarto was generally used with such alterations as had afterwards been made ; otherwise the playhouse manuscript was the text, and in some instances the prompter's notes have accidentally crept in. A few have been more carefully prepared, noticeably *Henry IV, Part II,* where all the Acts and scenes are marked ; but for the most part Acts are the only division and scenes are not noticed at all. Nor, with one or two exceptions, are there any place headings ; these were not added until 1709, when Rowe brought out the first ' edited ' Shakespeare.

Since Rowe, succeeding editors have modernized Shakespeare's spelling, use of capital letters, and punctuation, on the ground that the usage of the language has altered. But it has lately been pointed out by Mr. Percy Simpson that the capital letters and apparently casual punctuation in the Folio are not solely due to a light-hearted printer, but do in fact represent an entirely different system from our own. In other words, modern punctuation is used to explain the grammar of a sentence, whilst Shakespeare used the stops more freely—to show how a line should be spoken. Quite a good example is Antony's speech in *Julius Caesar,* first printed in the Folio, and as the errors are very few, obviously from a good original. If we read this passage (see opposite page), carefully observing the stops, and stressing the words in capital letters, and then compare it with the modern version, we can see how greatly the text has been changed for the worse by the editors.

*An.*Friends,Romans,Countrymen,lend me your ears:
I come to bury *Cæsar*,not to praife him :
The euill that men do, liues after them,
The good is oft enterred with their bones,
So let it be with *Cæsar*. The Noble *Brutus*,
Hath told you *Cæsar* was Ambitious :
If it were fo, it was a greeuous Fault,
And greeuoufly hath *Cæsar* anfwer'd it.
Heere, vnder leaue of *Brutus*,and the reſt
(For *Brutus* is an Honourable man,
So are they all;all Honourable men)
Come I to fpeake in *Cæsars* Funerall.
He was my Friend, faithfull,and iuſt to me ;
But *Brutus* fayes,he was Ambitious,
And *Brutus* is an Honourable man.
He hath brought many Captiues home to Rome,
Whofe Ranfomes, did the generall Coffers fill :
Did this in *Cæsar* feeme Ambitious ?
When that the poore haue cry'de, *Cæsar* hath wept :
Ambition fhould be made of ſterner ſtuffe,
Yet *Brutus* fayes, he was Ambitious :
And *Brutus* is an Honourable man.
You all did fee,that on the *Lupercall*,
I thrice prefented him a Kingly Crowne,
Which he did thrice refufe. Was this Ambition?
Yet *Brutus* fayes, he was Ambitious :
And fure he is an Honourable man.
I fpeake not to difprooue what *Brutus* fpoke,
But heere I am, to fpeake what I do know ;
You all did loue him once, not without caufe,
What caufe with-holds you then,to mourne for him?
O Iudgement ! thou are fled to brutifh Beaſts,
And Men haue loſt their Reafon. Beare with me,
My heart is in the Coffin there with *Cæsar*,
And I muſt pawfe,till it come backe to me.

Antony's speech in *Julius Caesar* (III. ii. 78), from the First Folio, 1623

Two more glaring examples of modernizing occur in the first Act of the same play. In Scene i, the stage direction of the Folio speaks of 'Commoners', and the dialogue is carried on by a 'Cobbler' and a 'Carpenter' who have been quite unnecessarily refined into '1st' and '2nd' 'Citizen'. The Folio marks no change of scene when all the characters have left the stage—of course there was none when the play was first acted—but simply adds the direction—

'Enter Caesar, Antony for the Course, Calphurnia, Portia, Decius, Cicero, Brutus, Cassius, Caska, a Soothsayer; after them Murellus and Flavius.'

This now reads in some editions:

'Scene 2. A Public Place. Enter in procession Caesar, Antony for the course, Calphurnia, Portia, Decius, Cicero, Brutus, Cassius and Casca; a great crowd following, among them a soothsayer.'

This wholly uncalled for improvement has entirely destroyed Shakespeare's subtle introduction of the tribunes, who have just left the stage but having fallen in with the procession are unwilling to join it, yet eager to see what will happen.

The Folio was reprinted in 1632, 1663–4, and 1685; each edition getting farther away from the original. Editors have tried to make things smooth for their readers by taking away whatever seemed rough in the original, and too often their method has been, as Dr. Johnson admitted, to 'tear what we cannot loose and eject what we happen not to understand'.